# I Hurt Too Much For A Band-Aid

## by Dr. Ken Olson

Author of the National Best Seller

The Art of Hanging Loose in an Uptight World by Dr. KEN OLSON

Featuring Psychological Exercises for Personal Growth

**HOLISTIC SOLUTIONS** to Physical and Emotional Pain.

Published by   O'SULLIVAN WOODSIDE & CO.
2218 East Magnolia
Phoenix, Arizona 85034

Manufactured in the United States of America.


First Edition, January 1980
Second Printing

Library of Congress Cataloging in Publication Data

Olson, Ken
   I Hurt too much for a band-aid.
    1. Pain, emotional and physical 2. Health—holistic solutions
79-6517
Publisher's ISBN: 0-89019-072-0
Follett T1410

To my Jeannie
for all her love,
belief and patience with me
throughout the years.

# Contents

# Preface

This book is a salute
to all the people who have experienced the pain of living,
but still have the courage
to fight for healing
and search for new answers
to health for the whole person.
The book is also the result of my own search
for the many answers to healing:
the power of the mind,
the chemistry of the body
and a philosophy of living.
This search is by no means complete, and the reader
is to understand that I don't have all the answers,
nor is there a finality to the facts
presented here.
It is too early to talk in terms of final truths and facts.
There is still too much not known.
The purpose of this book is
to help people assume responsibility
for their lives
and for their journey to health.

# Acknowledgements

I would like to acknowledge the dedication
and talented work of my editor, Helen Lovell.
A special thanks to Beverly Barker for her
contribution.

# 1

# I Hurt, I Really Hurt

There are no psychological diagnoses or psychiatric labels for hurt. One does not have to be psychotic or neurotic to hurt; no, one just has to be human. Pain is a fact of life. A newborn baby begins life with a slap on the bottom for the first cry. This should be a clue as to what is to follow! Sheldon Kopp has commented, "We all live in a tragic-comic situation; a life that is part absurd simply because it is not of our own making. We are born into a disordered world, into a family we did not choose, into circumstances we would have somewhat improved, and we are even called by a name we did not select."[1]

We are all raised by imperfect parents. Most of our parents were not trained and schooled in the art of raising children. Come to think of it though, some of the most troubled, messed-up children I have ever seen were raised by parents who were "trained" in the art of parenting, brought up in situations where one or both parents were either psychiatrists, psychologists or social workers. As a psychologist, I have found that it is much easier to wax eloquent to other parents about how they should raise their children than to practice what I preach in my own home. When I am home, my wife and children never do see me as the "all knowing psychologist," but, instead, they view me as "The Klutz," "Big Daddy," or "The Great White" (Whale). I realize the reason why I am not so impressive in their eyes is because they know me—and they still love me.

Being a parent is very stressful at times. For "on the spot" management of children, most parents do not recall the latest book or magazine article on "How to Be a Parent." Instead, they remember how their own parent or parents reacted in a similar situation. It's like the little kid who comes home from school with tears streaming down his face. His daddy says, "What happened, son?" and the little kid, between his hiccups and sobs, says, "Daddy, I got whipped, and I got beat up, and I got pushed

1. Sheldon Kopp, *If You Meet the Buddah on the Road, Kill Him!*(New York: Bantam Books, 1972)

1

down!" His dad, remembering his own dad's advice, says, "Well, you go out there and hit him back! I want you to go out like I did when I was your age and take it like a man." And the little kid looks up at his daddy and says, "All sixteen of 'em?"

Under the pressure of stress, if our own parents were physically abusive, then our route of action is the "beat a kid" psychology. When the stressful event has subsided, the parent will recall how much he hated the physical beatings, only to have that memory fail again in future punishments.

You don't have to be a psychologist to know that "all God's children got hang-ups." Because we are imperfect humans, we make mistakes all the time in the process of just living. It is this "fallability factor" that is very difficult for some of us to accept in ourselves. Rigid, authoritarian parents have a technique for hiding their own fallability factor from themselves: they set up high expectations for their children, demanding perfection as a means of proving to themselves that they are at least "good parents." In some instances this self-protective technique may work for a parent, but all too often it can destroy a child.

Leo Buscaglia tells of finding a book written by a girl named Michelle, who called her book *I Am Neither a Sacrilege Nor a Privilege, I May Not Be Competent or Excellent, But I Am Present.* Now that's a title! In her book, Michelle describes the agony of trying to measure up to the demands of perfection. She tells her mother:

> "My happiness is me, not you. Not only because you may be temporary, but also you want me to be what I am not. I cannot be happy when I change merely to satisfy you and your selfishness. Nor can I feel content when you criticize me for not thinking your thoughts or for not seeing like you. You call me a rebel. Yet each time I have rejected your beliefs, you have rebelled against mine. I do not try to mold your mind. I know you are trying hard enough to be just you and I cannot allow you to tell me what to be, for I am concentrating on being me. You said I was transparent and easily forgotten but why, then, did you try to use my lifetime to prove to yourself what you are? Why did you ask help from me when even *you* weren't on your side?" Michelle ends with, "I never did understand why you demanded perfection when you yourself are so imperfect."

Michelle was twenty years old when she drowned herself in the San Francisco Bay. After her death, her friends got together and published 500 copies of her book. In the forward they wrote, "Michelle, you were with us such a short time before choosing that fog-swept beach to continue on your personal way. It was July, 1967, and you were twenty."[2]

The happiest moments in my life have always been at the birth of a child into our family. If you are a parent yourself, you can recall those happy days. I recently experienced that same wonderful elation when my wife Jeannie and I flew to South Carolina to see our oldest son Mike, his wife "Cookie," and our first grandchild, Stephen Michael Olson. I shall never forget the spontaneous tears of joy that poured down Jeannie's face as Mike handed Stephen to her, and Cookie captured the moment with a picture. In my objective, scientific and completely unbiased opinion, he is the most beautiful baby boy in the world.

I wish our memories could recall those early days when as a baby each of us was a star, the prince or princess in the family. I wish we could remember how good it felt to be hugged and to know that the power of a cry would cause a big person to appear like magic to feed us, change our diapers, to hold us and whisper sweet words in our ears. If we could only again see those happy faces smiling down at us over our cribs, the faces with the silly grins, hoping for a big smile from us that wasn't just caused by gas. Boy, those were the days!

Unfortunately, those blissful days don't last a lifetime, because in the process of growing up, we soon experience a world of pain and hurt. We hear the angry voices of frustrated parents, we experience harsh words, spankings and punishments. The world is changed forever for the child. We get messges that we are never good enough or bright enough or right enough. When is enough, enough?

Ridicule? Think about those days in school; oh my, welcome to my nightmare! Some of those days were not filled with joy and pain, you know. They were just filled with pain. And if you think you had pain, listen with me to school kids all across our country today. They say, "You know, the reason why I don't go to the bathroom is not because I've got good bladder control. No, I'm gonna get stabbed and mugged!"

From the poem *Listen to the Children* comes this refrain:
> *Listen to the children when they cry.*
> *See the tears well up in their eyes and run*
>    *down their cheeks like warm drops of rain.*
> *They are learning the pain of not*
>    *being heard today*

2. Leo Buscaglia, "T.A.C.L.D. Presents Leo Buscaglia," (Texas: Texas Association for Children with Learning Disabilities, 1971)

> *Of hurting deep inside because no one*
> *thinks they're O.K.*[3]

There are so many hurts and pains experienced in the process of becoming an adult:

It hurts to feel that no matter what we do to please our parents, it is never enough.

It hurts to feel so shy, so unsure of ourselves. We want people to be our friends, but we are terrified of reaching out because of the possibility of rejection.

It hurts to have a physical handicap that causes people to stare, to even ridicule us because we're different. Being a little bit different hurts a lot.

It hurts to live with the fear of making mistakes because of the anger it incurs or the embarrassment it brings. The belief that "everything I do is wrong," hurts.

It hurts to be a teenager when our peers can be so cruel, competitive and cliquish. We face these challenges with a self-confidence so shaky that we wonder if we will ever survive our teens.

When the years roll around to love and marriage, we find two people who are filled with love, joy and great expectations for their future together. They get married "for better or for worse," and sometimes it's worse than they thought. As the years race by, numerous couples painfully discover that love doesn't conquer all. In time, too many marriages are hurting because of emotional starvation, boredom and bitterness. They begin to live together as strangers, afraid to open up to real intimacy for fear of being hurt. Loneliness stalks their marriages. Deepest needs are hidden behind protective masks and games. So alone, and yet together.

Eugene Kennedy wrote:

> The worst thing about pain is that it doesn't kill us. We never die of pain, although we sometimes wish that we could, if only to put an end to it. And the worst pains are those which seem to have no remedies, the ones that tear the edges of our spirit because they come when we are healthy rather than when we are sick. We may try to tranquilize these pains away, but eventually the ache returns. They even go on vacations with us, waiting for an idle moment or a familiar song to use as entrance into our hearts. What is this pain that will not kill us, this ache that has learned how to follow us so slowly through life? It is the pain of being alive, the pain of always having to face a new challenge, the pain

3. Ken Olson, *The Art of Hanging Loose in an Uptight World* (Phoenix, Arizona: O'Sullivan Woodside & Co., 1974) (hereafter cited as *The Art of Hanging Loose*)

4

of wanting love, and the pain of finding it, the ache of starting again when we don't feel like it, the tension of coming to terms with a life that keeps shifting under our feet.[4]

Could I ask you to stop for a moment and go inside yourself to the memory banks of your mind, to recall some of your past hurts? I don't want this to be just a book filled with facts, but rather a conversation between you and me. I want you to experience this book by gaining practical insights into yourself, instead of simply reading it. In the recalling of old hurts and pains of yesteryear, you have permission to shed a few tears. Just shut the book, close your eyes and allow those early memories to become very vivid and real.

It's amazing how we think those old memories of pain are forgotten, until we become flooded with the power and vividness of recollection. Maybe right now you are saying, "Who needs this book? I was feeling pretty good before I started reading this, and now I'm hurting and depressed by those old memories. Thanks a lot, Ken!" Please bear with me! This book is not just about hurts, but about healing and living. How you deal with the suffering of the past is very important. Pain is often a way of informing us that we have some unfinished business of yesterday. Whenever you get a headache it doesn't mean that your body has suddenly developed an aspirin deficiency, but that something is out of harmony in your body. The pain gets your attention! So, instead of rushing to numb the pain, stop and listen to what your hurts and pains are trying to tell you.

I've had lots of seminars with small groups of people learning to get in touch with their painful memories. Most of them soon discover that their private pain and hurt is also their common bond of experience with everyone else. In one seminar for married couples, a young wife began to cry, the tears flowing down her cheeks like a waterfall. Her husband held her tight in his arms. I asked her if she wanted to share with the group or just keep it to herself. Through her sobs and tears, she began to describe a very tragic experience that happened one night when she was seven years old.

"My parents took me to a large company picnic, and when we were crossing the road, I saw a truck rushing toward us at a high speed, weaving down the road as if the driver was drunk. I ran to the other side of the road and then looked back to see both of my parents killed by the truck."

There was a rush of tears and sobbing before she could go on

4. Eugene Kennedy, *The Pain of Being Human* (Chicago: The Thomas Moore Press, 1972)

5

any further. "I never realized until today," she said haltingly, "that I had blocked out so many of the memories, and that I had not resolved the pain."

I asked her what else hurt, and if she could remember what she did that night. "I went for help," she said. "I remember now, I went back to the big ballroom where everyone was dancing, and I tried to get someone to listen to me, and it was as if nobody seemed to care that my mother and father had just been killed. They just kept on dancing and partying. Nobody stopped to touch me, to hold me or wipe away my tears. That nobody cared what had happened to me, really hurt. It was amazing."

After she told us her painful story, she began to realize how much she needed to be at that seminar, and how good it felt to be surrounded by a group of people who cared and could cry with her and comfort her. Now it was time to make the decision that she had hurt long enough. It was time to put a period on the pain.

This woman later said that she had no idea that she would reveal this private pain to a group of people, but when she did reveal her burden, she found so much acceptance and love that she felt relieved from the huge load she had been carrying around all those years. She began to realize that the suffering of the past was like stored-up, destructive energy, which needed to be released in order that she might be set free. The troubles and disillusionments of life have a way of being like parasites, hanging on our energy and robbing us of our enthusiasm for living. Do you have some unfinished business with the heartaches of yesterday? Isn't it time to let go of them? How long are you going to hurt? It's time to put a period on the pain.

Sometimes there can come into our lives a pain so devastating that we are knocked down and overwhelmed. We are filled with such anguish that we cry as if there is no bottom to the well of tears. We find ourselves sobbing intensely, our bodies shaking and convulsing. Our minds are a blur, filled with racing thoughts and flashing pictures. We feel endless bewilderment because what has happened makes no sense. It seems like the nightmares during our few hours of sleep stretch into our days of wakefulness. We lose strength and acquire feelings of helplessness. We feel a sense of rising panic, realizing that we are holding on to the edge of life by our fingernails. From the depths of our being, we cry out in anguish for help.

If you have ever hurt this intensely, the pain can become so devastating that you desperately reach out for someone to hear your pain, your cry for help. If only someone would accept your tears, hold you until you stop shaking, and comfort you simply with their presence, because there are no right or clever words to say. It is enough that this person is with you in your darkest hour.

The tragedy is that too often, when you reach out in desperation to another person, they back away and offer a band-aid to patch up your hurt and pain. Band-aids of platitudes such as:

> God only gives to a person what that person can handle.
> Give yourself time, because time heals all wounds.
> You have to look at the bright side. You could become a better person for this.
> Come on now, pull yourself together. You've got to be brave—be strong.
> Take a Valium.
> Have a stiff drink.
> Take three aspirin.
> In time you will understand that this is God's will.
> Other people have even worse problems. You should be thankful.

I'm not exactly sure what scares the "band-aid" people so much. Maybe it's the intensity of the suffering person's pain. It could be the experience of the impotence of not knowing what to do or say. Perhaps it is the fear that a similar pain could come into their own lives (maybe it's catching?) that freaks people out, causing them to withdraw and run from the scene of the pain. How useless it is to try to cover up a deep, gaping hurt with a band-aid platitude! When a person is hurting that much, he doesn't want any platitudes; it is at that time he wants to scream out, "I hurt too much for a band-aid!"

A deeply troubled woman made an appointment with a psychiatrist. He asked her what her problem was, and she reported that she was so depressed and—before she could finish her statement, the physician whipped out his pad and wrote her prescriptions for her depression and for sleeping pills. The woman was furious. She wadded up the prescriptions, threw them at the psychiatrist and screamed, "You idiot! If you had let me finish telling you why I was so depressed, I would have told you that I am a prescription drug addict. I take up to twenty Seconals a day, and you give me *more* drugs! Why don't you *listen?*" With that, she stormed out of the office!

But then, she did a very foolish and dangerous thing. With the help of her husband, staying with her day and night, she "cold turkeyed" from her drugs. After she began her withdrawl, for three weeks she was vulnerable to convulsions and death. When she and her husband showed up at my office for an appointment, I told them what a dangerous thing she had done, but that I could understand her frustration and anger. She hurt so much, but because the psychiatrist wasn't listening, she was given a band-aid.

The most painful experience of my life, which still hurts to talk about, occurred in January of 1970. I was coming home from a group therapy session at my office, around 10:30 p.m. As I passed a car on the right, I saw a figure in a black jacket walking across the road. He was walking from the side of the street with an open field, and crossing in the middle of the block. I hit the brakes, blew my horn and headed toward the curb, but the person walked right into my car. There was a sickening thud, and the man was killed. I called the police and ambulance from what turned out to be the man's own home. It was later found out that he had been drinking, and the cabbie that had picked him up from the bar put him out on the opposite side of the street, when all he had to do was to turn into his driveway and let him out. It was even against the law to stop on that side of the street. It was declared an unavoidable accident, but I had to drive home looking through my smashed windshield. My Jeannie and my children helped comfort me through my tears and sobs.

The pain of the accident was so intense that I called the pastor of the church that I belonged to then, but he couldn't hear my painful struggle. I turned to a close friend to share the agony I was experiencing, but all I got was a band-aid. Two nights after the accident, I was conducting a group therapy session for dope fiends and drug abusers—messed up teen-agers. One of those kids looked at me and said, "Doc, how ya handlin' the hurt?" I found acceptance that night. I found love and a ministry of healing. No band-aids were offered; I hurt too much for a band-aid.

# 2

# The Destructiveness of Guilt

Would you like to live in a world free of guilt? Before you eagerly say, "Yes!" let me give you a small glimpse of what a guilt-free world would be like. The years I spent working in the drug culture revealed a world with no sense of guilt, no values or morals. It was an uptight, paranoid world of no trust; a jungle of the "riper" and the "ripee." A dope fiend did not consider himself a criminal even though he lied, cheated, stole, robbed, dealt drugs, and even at times killed, to support his drug habit. In 1970, it was estimated that one heroin addict, supporting his drug habit by illegal means, cost the community about $50,000 a year. (Just think what that would be now, with inflation!)

One day, during those years, I was listening to a very angry young man in a juvenile detention center. He was upset because someone there had stolen something of his. He was filled with righteous indignation against the unknown thief. I asked him why he was in juvenile detention, and he said, "For stealing"! His only sense of right and wrong was the wrong that was done to him.

A dope fiend, when confronted with his criminal behavior, will immediately blame his parents, society, the establishment, the police and anyone else he can think of, because it is *always* someone else's fault; surely he is not to blame or guilty of anything! Consequently, the major goal of therapy with this "guilt-less" person is to bluntly confront him with feedback about his behavior. He needs to learn the consequences of his acts and develop a new value structure.

The "blaming game" is as old as man, it is so much a part of being human, that the story of Adam and Eve and their disobedience is classic. God asked Adam why he ate the fruit of the tree of the knowledge of good and evil, and Adam quickly blamed not only Eve, but God, for his action. He said, "It was the woman *you* gave me. She made me do it." Eve was not to be outdone. When she was asked by God why she disobeyed, she quickly

9

responded, "It was that snake in the grass that talked me into it. It's his fault." Flip Wilson echoes Eve's sentiments with "the devil made me do it."

Modern psychiatry and psychology have a strong tendency to "psychoanalyze" a person's guilt away, so that whatever is wrong is not his fault. In T.S. Elliot's *A Cocktail Party,* Celia tells Reilly the psychiatrist, "Well, my bringing up was pretty conventional. I had always been taught to disbelieve in sin. Oh, I don't mean that it was never mentioned! But any wrong, from our point of view, was either bad form or was psychological."[1]

The value of guilt lies in giving us messages that we have done something wrong, and thus raises within us a tension that becomes a strong stimulus to rectify the wrong, or at least ask forgiveness of the person wronged. Even though it is painful to a person's pride to go to a wronged party and seek forgiveness, the very act of confession is beneficial to the person experiencing the guilt, because it allows the discharge of the negative, destructive energy of guilt. Thus, confession is a valuable release and relief. Confession is also healthful for the person who has been hurt, because in the granting of forgiveness, the healing of the hurt can be completed. Forgiveness is an eraser which wipes the slate clean. To say, "I'll forgive you, but I'll never forget what you've done," is not forgiveness, nor will the healing of the hurts ever be finished.

The destructiveness of guilt lies in experiencing the feeling of guilt, but not knowing what you have done wrong to feel guilty about. The contamination of this false guilt can be very destructive. Have you ever realized how deeply we are programmed to feel guilty about ourselves? For example, how often do you have four or five good days in a row and, as a result, feel nervous about it, because you don't "deserve" these good days, and surely something terrible is going to happen to you! To break the tension of "guilt" you fight with a family member or do something else to "blow it," because of the belief that you really don't deserve good days.

A graphic example of the results of the contamination of guilt within a family took place in a therapy session with a family of one girl and two boys. The daughter, who was twenty years old at the time, turned to her father and said, "What must I do to win your approval? I did everything you wanted me to in high school. I was on the honor roll all four years. I was class officer each year. I was the president of the Campus Crusade for Christ

1. T.S. Eliot, *The Complete Poems and Plays* (New York: Harcourt, Brace & Co., 1934)

chapter." She went on to pour out her numerous achievements, and then she said, "And I'm even a good artist!"

Her father broke in, "Since when are you an artist!"

"I know," she sobbed. "I had to keep something for myself. If I had shown you my art work, you would have contaminated it by pointing out what was wrong with it." Then the tears flowed as if the dam was broken.

If you are a woman, how often have you felt that no matter how many things you accomplish in a day, it is never good enough? Advertizements in magazines and on television portray such a perfectly put-together woman that, well, any woman less than that feels guilty.

A large percentage of the work force consists of married women. I believe the number of working wives is not so much due to women's liberation as it is to the need to combat the high cost of living. No matter how much a working wife and mother does an excellent job of balancing her responsibilities, the specter of guilt still haunts her.

The events which lead to this undercurrent of guilt can be illustrated in a typical scene: Mom comes home from work to a husband and children who have gotten there before she did. She no sooner gets in the doorway, and before she has time to put down her purse, her husband says, "Honey, would you get me a beer?" As she goes to the refrigerator muttering to herself, "Why can't he get his own beer?" she is met by two of her children with, "Mommy, you have to go talk to the principal in the morning!" and, "Mom, I told my home room teacher you would make four dozen brownies for our party tomorrow." She finds herself screaming at the children to get out of the kitchen, and, as she rushes into the family room with her husband's beer, she feels guilty and thinks, "What a terrible mother I am." She shoves the beer at her husband, with a look that could kill, and stalks off to fix supper. Suddenly, in all the rushing around, feeling like she has to serve, be the martyr and be all things to everyone, she finds herself slowly burning inside. "When is it going to be my turn?"

The tragedy of this illustration is that it is too true, and that the woman doesn't see that there is another way; and there *is* another way. She could have come home with a recognition of her own needs and said, "Husband, if you want a beer, help yourself, unless your legs are both broken." And, "Kids, nobody's going to die in the next fifteen minutes. I will not listen to any problems or make any decisions until I have had a shower

11

and lain down for fifteen minutes. There will be some mellow music playing in my room and a "Do Not Disturb" sign on the door. I'm doing this for myself, so I won't end up being the witch of the night."

Now if the average mother really did this, she would probably end up in the shower feeling guilty and thinking, "What would Mother think of my being so selfish? I should be loving to my husband. I should be a better mother. Since I'm working now, I wonder if my children could be pre-delinquent?" Then, trying to rest on the bed and listen to relaxing music, she thinks, "I wonder how long I have to stay here and relax?"

It's amazing how many mothers feel guilty if they take time for themselves alone. After hearing me mention in a seminar the need for time alone, a woman approached me the next day and told me that she realized that she had no time for herself and had made a decision to give herself one hour a week. I was curious as to what hour she chose, and she told me that, after much thought, she had selected the hour between 2 and 3 a.m. each Thursday, just for herself. If she could only remember to wake up at that hour, it would be all hers!

As a family therapist, I find it frightening to see how guilt and fear are so destructively used to control the lives of children. In some families there is a family "scapegoat," who is the focus of blame and guilt in the family. Degrees of destructiveness to the scapegoated child can range from one where the child has no right to be different, to the extreme where the child has no right to *be*.

For my doctoral dissertation I did a study entitled, "An Investigation of Scapegoating, Favoritism and Self-Blame in Families."[2] The research was conducted at the Arizona State Hospital Children's Psychiatric Unit. I especially wanted to study the scapegoating and self-blaming activities of the families that had resulted in one of their children being admitted to the State Hospital. Researchers in family therapy have long recognized this phenomenon, which is a major problem in the dysfunctional family unit: one in which a family scapegoat is needed to be the focus of blame in the family, in order to keep the rest of the family members from going crazy.

In my research, the task given each family member was to write out on separate cards what they felt was the major virtue of self and of each family member, and the major fault of self and of each family member. Afterwards, and all the cards of faults and

2. Ken Olson, "An Investigation of Scapegoating, Favoritism and Self-Blame in Families." (Ph.D. diss., Arizona State University, 1968)

virtues were shuffled. I would then read the statement on each card, and each family member would write down on a sheet of paper who they believed each statement pertained to in the family.

I will never forget how in one large family, the hospitalized teenager kept saying after each blame statement was read, "I know who that one belongs to." After the answers were tallied and the results were in, it was evident that he had ascribed all the blame statements to himself. He was the family scapegoat, the family "blame blotter."

The results of the research, which was exploratory in nature, tended to show that the disturbed child is the child least favored by the family individuals. As a result of the scapegoating, the disturbed child in a family perceives himself as primarily the one who is guilty for the trouble and disturbance within the family. The disturbed child seems to internalize the family's projection of blame, and thus sees himself as the "sacrificial victim" who must be punished to save the family. Unfortunately, the disturbed child in a family is not accurate in his perceptions of the other family members. Thus, the family scapegoat not only feels intense guilt over what actually was his fault, but also absorbs blame for that which was not even his responsibility.

Another strategy used by parents to control the lives of their children is, "What Will the Neighbors Think?" Better be careful about what you do, because the neighbors are watching you. If you do something even a little bit naughty, why, all the neighbors will gossip about what a bad person you are, and this will reflect on the family name. In the past, this has often proven to be an effective control of behavior, but as we have become a nation of gypsies, always on the move, the moral control by the community has broken down. As a result, a person doesn't worry anymore about what the neighbors will think, because probably the neighbors don't care; in fact, we most likely don't even *know* our neighbors.

However, the fear of disapproval by others is still with us in many ways. For example, if company is coming for dinner, the little lady of the house not only plans an excellent meal and cleans the house with a fury, but she also runs out to the grocery store for a few more things. The "fun" evening of entertaining produces an exhausted, frazzled woman, who manages to shower and get dressed just before the company arrives. The guests compliment her on how *nice* the house looks, and what

13

does she say? "Oh, but if you only knew how the storage room looks. What a mess!"

Now what *will* they think of her, since she has a dirty, unkempt storage room? It will come as a shock to her, and possibly to you too, that people do not spend much time thinking about you. They are busy thinking about themselves and what kind of impression they will make. Relieved?

I wonder how many people grow up under the fear and control of "be careful of what *they* say, or what *they* think." Someday I'm going to write a book titled, "In Search of They." What *they* say has so much power over our lives. Once, I even looked for a Library of Society in Washington, D.C., where I felt sure all the *theys* would be recorded. Needless to say, it was a fruitless search.

An excellent and very funny book about guilt is *How to Be a Jewish Mother,* by Dan Greenburg. Of course, it's important to note that all Jewish mothers aren't Jewish. This is a handbook on how to make guilt work for you. In the section on "Practice Drills" are the following suggestions:

> (1) Give your son Marvin two sportshirts as a present. The first time he wears one of them, look at him sadly and say in Basic Tone of Voice, "The other one you didn't like?"

> (2) Borrow a tape recorder and practice the following key phrases until you can deliver them with eye-watering perfection: (a) Go ahead and enjoy yourself. (b) But be careful. (c) Don't worry about me. (d) I don't mind staying home alone. (e) I'm glad it happened to me and not you.

> (3) Remember the child is an unformed, emotionally unstable, ignorant creature. To make him feel secure you must continually remind him of the things which you are denying yourself on his account, especially when others are present.[3]

One morning, Jeannie and I were having breakfast at the Royal Hawaiian Hotel in Waikiki. We could not help overhearing two widows in their 80's talking. Another couple on their tour came over to exchange pleasantries with them. As they left the table, one of them said to the two widows, "Now, don't get into any trouble!" One of the widows responded, "Couldn't you just have said, 'Have fun'?"

To live under the control of fear is to live under a cruel tyrant. Dostoyevsky once remarked, "More things are done because of fear, and more things remain undone as a result of fear than any other emotion. Now if we strike fear in favor of love, if what we

3. Dan Greenburg, *How to Be a Jewish Mother* (Los Angeles: Price, Stern and Sloan Inc., 1964)

did and did not was promoted by love instead of fear, we would glimpse the potential which all of us share."

It seems to me that far too often religions have used fear to control the lives of the followers. Fear and guilt have, unfortunately, been the motivation in a person's struggle to be "good." To further aid in the effectiveness of guilt, religions have developed rules and laws which become more important than God's words on how to live. Since I have my orientation in the Christian faith, I have noticed that too often God is pictured as a "cosmic killjoy," who snoops around looking for Christians who are having fun, so he can put an end to it. As a result of this misconception, there is so little joy, so little love. In the early Christian Church, the outsiders would often remark, "Look at those Christians, how they love one another." Can the same be said today? No, I'm afraid that it would be more accurate to say, "Look at those dull Christians and how they gossip about each other."

I firmly believe that churches make people feel guilty about the wrong things and not about the right things. People are more concerned with keeping man-made rules, than in loving and forgiving. In their positions of the "keepers of the rules," they forget about reaching out to those who are guilty and hurting. They forget about inviting them to come meet a loving God and Savior, who will wipe the slate clean with forgiveness, and will remember their sins no more.

One of the first decisions in diffusing the destructiveness of guilt is to accept the fact that *we are human*. Guilt can become like a cancer that slowly and methodically destroys us. It can rob us of the joy of living and color our world in shades of grey. Too often, when we are suffering from guilt, we become our own judge and jury and even self-inflict the pain of punishment. Self-forgiveness is not even considered as an option. Forgiveness by God is denied, because we feel if God really knew us he wouldn't forgive us. It is quite the reverse, my friend; God does know you and does forgive those who ask it. Stop and think; maybe the basis for refusing forgiveness is the failure to accept our humanness. Man is born to goof. No one is perfect.

One day, an honor roll student in his junior year in high school was admitted to a psychiatric hospital in which I was conducting group therapy for young adults. Jerry was experiencing the terrifying, living nightmare of a bad trip on L.S.D. He "knew" he was dead, and the sound of a tractor working outside convinced him that his grave was being prepared.

15

Over the days, I tried to encourage Jerry to try living—even if it meant only going swimming in the pool. He steadfastly refused, because he believed there were poisonous rays coming out of his body, which would poison the water and kill anyone else in the pool. As he was heavily medicated with Thorazine, he was like a zomby in group therapy.

About a week after admission to the hospital, Jerry began to regress and lost his ability to walk. Another week later he lost his ability to talk. Soon after that, he could no longer control his bowel and bladder, so he was put in large diapers. It took no keen, analytical thinking to realize that in a short time Jerry would be dead. You can only regress so far.

One day, motivated by the desperateness of the situation, I sat down on the floor where Jerry was crawling around, looked him straight in the eye, and said, "It's time to forgive yourself for taking acid. It's time to quit punishing yourself for blowing your mind. It's time to start living *now*." Over and over I repeated these words to Jerry.

The next day, he walked into group therapy and talked. We were all amazed at his recovery. A nurse asked him what had happened, and Jerry repeated what I had said to him the day before. When asked how many times he had repeated that to himself, Jerry replied, "About 10 to 20 thousand times."

I wonder how many people need to hear and repeat these words in order to be free of the destructive power of guilt:

It's time to forgive myself.

It's time to quit punishing myself.

It's time to start living *now*.

# 3

# The Death of a Relationship

It feels so good to be loved! Is that why it hurts so much when love is gone, and a relationship dies? There are no pain thermometers to measure the awesome power and intensity of the pain a person experiences during the traumatic time of the loss of a loved one. This loss from the death of a relationship is felt in the breaking up of young lovers, by people going through a divorce, by those ending a significant involvement, and by people experiencing the death of a loved one.

I have been struck by the varying emotions mirrored in the faces of people in times of personal catastrophes: a newspaper picture of a parent holding a dead child reveals a face filled with raw anguish and grief, but a picture of a couple looking at the complete destruction of their home by a tornado reveals faces of stunned disbelief and despair. The striking differences reveal that you can replace things, but you can't replace a dead loved one.

A woman in therapy described her personal hell to me by saying:

> I lived with the pain of rejection, and the cruelty of the fact that a man I had loved for twenty-five years had been unfaithful to our marriage. It was sickening to realize that our relationship had been a lie from his point of view. Finally, all my tears stopped, for the tear ducts had run dry. After that came a violent, terrible pain that caused hours of retching. There were no pills powerful enough, no words comforting enough; all was anger, bitterness, hate, disbelief. In spite of all this, there was one even more cruel emotion: *hope*; even after all the hurt, I found I couldn't stop loving that man after all those years. The pain of *hopeless hope* was so intense that at times I wanted to die.

People actually do die of broken hearts, although I have never seen a death certificate which listed the cause of death as a broken heart, grief or loneliness. Colin Parkes, in his book

*Bereavement Studies in Grief in Adult Life*, points out the vulnerability of a person when a deep, personal love is suddenly and permanently taken away. This shattering loss of love is costly.

Parkes points out that the increased mortality rate among the grief stricken is especially high during the first six months after the loss of a loved one through death. This finding is revealing, because it shows that the increase in mortality in widows and widowers is not due to the fact that these individuals were unable to remarry and rebuild their lives. The increase in sudden deaths occured before sufficient time for remarriage had elapsed. It is startling to note that the cause of death in 75% of the cases Parkes studied was from coronary thrombosis or arteriosclerosis.[1]

The grief reaction for those who suffer the loss of a relationship other than through death is often one of increased vulnerability to suicide. Thoughts turn to suicide when the person realizes that no matter what he does, no matter how much he hopes and dreams, nothing will bring back the loved one. Life appears worthless; why not end the pain?

Experts who study suicide report that suicide as a result of lost love ranks with heart disease and cancer as a cause of death. Suicide prevention centers in the U.S. report that nearly 80% of the cases they come in contact with involve a loss of love.[2] Reports also show that the incredibly high suicide rate among teenagers can almost be exclusively caused by the loss of a relationship.

James Lynch has made an extensive study of the effects of the death of a relationship in his book *The Broken Heart*. The purpose of his book is to demonstrate that human companionship does affect our hearts; that there is reflected in our hearts a biological basis for our need for loving human relationships, which we fail to fulfill at our peril. Since human dialogue is the elixer of life, the ultimate decision we must make is simple: we either learn to live together successfully or increase our chances of prematurely dying—alone.

Lynch, in his studies on the premature death rates for men and women who experience the loss of a spouse, either by death or divorce, reports the following:

> For divorced, widowed and single men, both white and non-white, the overall death rates for cardiovascular disease were two

1. Colin Parkes, *Bereavement: Studies of Grief in Adult Life* (New York: International Universities Press, 1972)

2. Zev Wanderer and Tracy Cabot, *Letting Go* (New York: G.P. Putnam's Sons, 1978)

to three times higher than for married men. Similar trends were also true for women. For almost every other major cause of premature death there were also marked increases for the non-married over the married, with differences in death rates as high as tenfold. Death rates for heart disease, motor vehicle accidents, cancer of the respiratory system, cancer of the digestive organs, stroke, suicide, cirrhosis of the liver, rheumatic fever, hypertension, pneumonia, diabetes, homicide, tuberculosis—all these were higher among single, widowed and divorced individuals.[3]

Somewhere along the way, the Heart Association should focus its attention not only on the role of exercise, the benefits of low-fat diets, and the dangers of smoking in the prevention of heart attack, but also on the shape of American marriages and family life. The heart has long been the symbol of love. The loss of love can affect our hearts, and without love we die.

The awareness of deep needs and human vulnerability in the breaking up of a relationship is graphically revealed in the slow and painful deaths of most marriages through the process of divorce. I have not had the experience of counseling people through those reasonable, dignified, "bloodless" divorces, where people painlessly terminate their marriages. The divorces I have worked with have been painful, vengeful, ugly, tragic and devastating; of course, my sample could be explained by the fact that only those who were having a terrible time sought professional help. It is also true that for some people a divorce is not a traumatic experience, but a feeling of relief that "it is all over."

Even though the divorce rate is climbing and couples divorcing are common, it does not follow that we are accepting and adjusting to divorce any better. Divorce is still rated as one of the three most serious emotional traumas a person can experience. The death of a relationship through a divorce is an emotional crisis of major magnitude. If there are any children in the family, it is not only the divorce of two people, but the divorce of a family that will never be the same again.

The stages of grief experienced by those who lose a loved one through death are also experienced by those who go through a divorce. Elizabeth Kubler-Ross, in her book *On Death and Dying,* describes these five stages of the grief process as denial, anger, bargaining, depression and, finally, acceptance.[4]

For the person undergoing a divorce, the first stage comes as a general feeling of unreality. There is a dialogue going on inside that person which says, "No, not me! Divorce is something that

3. James J. Lynch, *The Broken Heart* (New York: Basic Books, Inc., 1977) (hereafter cited as *The Broken Heart*)

4. Elizabeth Kubler-Ross, *On Death and Dying* (New York: MacMillan, 1970)

happens to people in the 'soaps' on T.V. or in the movies. It might even happen to the Smiths next door, but surely I'm not going to find my name in that cold, grim 'Divorces Granted' column in the newspaper."

Next, after the discussions of "who keeps what" are over, the marriage partner moves out, and the reality of that first night alone hits; that other person just isn't going to be in the same house anymore. I have talked with men who have struggled with the aloneness of divorce, men who find themselves living in a smaller place with nothing of their own. One man called his apartment "The Lonely Pit." He finally bought a cheap painting to hang on the wall, so there would be something of his own.

The feelings of unreality and aloneness are shattering, but they are soon followed by the even more powerful emotions of anger and bitterness. Self cries out, "It's not fair. Why me?" The person is flooded with rage and self-pity, mixed with guilt and remorse over what "might have been." Emotions surge with such intensity that some people become frightened of their responses. They feel like they are in shock. Food is tasteless, if not repulsive. Self-identity becomes a problem. Fear of the unknown is overpowering. Concerns about the children are overwhelming.

The intensity of the grief reaction to the breaking-up of the relationship is in direct proportion to the length of the marriage, and the way the person perceives himself in the goal of shaping and directing the family. Suddenly, the person realizes how the marriage and the family and, yes, even the house, were key reference points of identity. In this regards, men are often shocked to see the marriage and family in a new light. Formerly it was easy to say, "I'll work hard and put off doing things with the kids, but someday it will be different." Yet, as one man said, "It's real different, all right. Now I'm in Arizona, and my wife and young children are in New York—for good."

Dependency needs on the partner for completion of a personal life are now painfully recognized. The emotional turmoil involved in making the decision to divorce prevents many women from thinking about the stark economic realities they will face after the divorce. Ironically, money problems may have been a major factor in precipitating a divorce, but now the money problems turn into a financial disaster. The nice house has to be sold, there is a step down in social standing, luxuries are no longer possible, and making ends meet, especially with children, becomes impossible. Two separate households are definitely more expensive than one. If the wife, who has formerly devoted her energies to being a homemaker, looks for employment, she will find the prospects grim. Discrimination against women is very real when it comes to paycheck time.

It is at this point where couples who are separated often reach the bargaining stage of "let's make a deal" and try it one more time. Usually one member of the relationship was not so enthusiastic about getting a divorce in the first place. Hope for a reconciliation begins. Painful times are forgotten and pleasant times recalled. In this stage of bargaining, seeing the marriage partner and children can fill a person with a mixture of love and hate, hope and depression. In time, one or both realize that there will be no reconciliation, no remarriage to each other. The final hope is extinguished.

For the one who held out the hope that things would work out, there comes a black despair, an overwhelming depression. The grief and tears of helplessness are so overpowering that the person wonders if he can go on. Yet, out of that darkest time there comes one day, in some small way, the dawning of the realization that the reality of the divorce has been accepted. The knowledge that "Hey, I made it" comes. "I was not destroyed. I learned something about myself. I can make it after all." The person is then able to put a period on the relationship.

Of course, it is necessary to note that these emotional reactions in divorce do not always follow the four stages of grief, but the pain of the death of a relationship is very real. It hurts too much for a band-aid.

# 4

# I'm So Lonely I Could Die

After a person has gone through the very painful death of a relationship and made it back to the land of the living, there comes a time of decision between two choices. The first choice is to go out and develop new, meaningful relationships and get on with the living of it. The second choice is to withdraw into the protective shell of aloneness, and vow to never be hurt like that again. Loneliness is safe, but it is a slow death on the installment plan. The decision not to love again means that, to a degree, a person dies.

Early in life most of us learn about the stove in our mother's kitchen. We found out that when we put our fingers on it, we got burned. We seldom forget that first experience of being burned, and we make a decision that we sure won't let that happen again. The pain of our burned fingers made a lasting imprint in the memory banks of our minds. From the pain we learned.

So it is with our experiences with people. There isn't anybody that hasn't been burned by other people. And the pain of that experience sometimes helps us to make a decision about people. Will we be vulnerable and dare to reach out again? Will we touch again, love again? Maybe we will instead make a decision to retreat. We run across the planks of our own private moat, draw up the bridge and put the bar across the door. We sit securely in our castle, safe from outward invasion. But soon our castle becomes our prison—dull, grey, cold and lifeless.

One time I attended a Seven Step program at the Arizona State Prison. I went there as a "Square John," someone from the straight world who was coming to offer hope and encouragement to the prisoners and help them try to get their lives in order. While I was there, a first timer to the Seven Step meeting went to the podium and told his story. He told us in a boastful manner that he was indeed a very good burglar, and that he had done thirty-three years of prison time in various states. I stood up and told him that he was a lousy burglar, and that he had no talent for crime. I clarified myself by telling him that every time he left a prison he would pull another job and get busted again, because he could not handle the responsibility of freedom and caring for himself. He had left the responsibility for his life up to the state. Thirty-three years of prisons has made *his* world a better place! I suggested only one improvement on his plans. He could pick the next state by its climate, pull a job there, get busted and go to prison where the weather suited his tastes. He sheepishly admitted that what I said was true.

One of the most difficult things to face is that we are responsible for our own loneliness. We don't want to face our accountability for loneliness. It is the one truth we want to avoid at all costs. It's so much easier to slip into a quagmire of self-pity and helplessly wallow around in it. It's always the other fellow's fault; other people let us down, rejected us, hurt us. Life is unfair, so why should we set ourselves up for a fall! These, and countless other reasons, are given for the loneliness that somehow engulfs us like a fog in the night. Loneliness, according to most of us, just happens.

One very bright, moonlit night, I was flying over Texas and looking at the small towns lit up below me. As I gazed down on all the homes, I began to wonder what was going on in each of them. How many couples were quarreling? How many homes were filled with love? How many people were living out another too quiet, lonely evening in front of the T.V. set? The awareness of the possibility of so many lonely lives in the homes spread out below me was overwhelming. Leo Rosten's words came to me, "Everyone is lonely at the bottom, and cries out to be understood, but we can never really understand anyone else. We remain part strangers even to those who love us."

The following Sunday we sang a hymn at our Folk Worship Service that not only described the experiences of other people's loneliness, but my own as well:

> *Lonely voices crying in the city,*
> *Lonely voices sounding like a child.*
> *Lonely voices come from busy people*
> *Too disturbed to stop a little while.*
> *Lonely voices fill my dreams,*
> *Lonely voices haunt my memory.*
>
> *Lonely faces looking for the sunrise,*
> *Just to find another busy day.*
> *Lonely faces all around a city,*

*Men afraid, but too ashamed to pray.*
*Lonely faces do I see,*
*Lonely faces haunt my memory.*

*Lonely eyes, I see them in the subway,*
*Burdened by the worries of the day.*
*Men at leisure, but they're so unhappy,*
*Tired of foolish roles they try to play.*
*Lonely people do I see,*
*Lonely people haunt my memory.*

*Abundant life He came to truly give man,*
*But so few His gift of grace receive.*
*Lonely people live in every city,*
*Men who face a dark and lonely grave.*
*Lonely faces do I see,*
*Lonely voices calling out to me.*[1]

Loneliness is a common experience to all of us, yet, by its very nature, it is a profoundly private reality, full of raw sensitivity and pain. The pain of loneliness can become so intense that we inwardly cry out, "Doesn't anybody hear me hurting? How could anyone *not* see this painful loneliness!" But they don't. I think that somewhere along the line, in the experience of loneliness, each of us becomes aware that we are solitary, unique individuals, whose deepest fears and hopes may never really be fully shared with another person.

When our daughter Jan was ready to start high school, I wanted to have a father-daughter talk with her about being a teenager. When I approached the subject, I was shocked to hear her say, "Dad, you're too late."

"What do you mean?" I asked anxiously.

"Mike and Danny have already had a talk with me about boys, sex and getting along in high school."

Apparently I had been upstaged by my two sons, but I was amazed to hear the final words of wisdom each brother had given to Jan. They said (unbeknown to each other), "Jan, you're a very beautiful girl, and we're proud of you as our sister. In high school you will have to make a decision between being popular and going along with the crowd, or being your own person. If you decide to be your own person, then you will have to come to terms with paying the price of loneliness."

I was amazed at this "heavy" advice Mike and Danny had given their fourteen-year-old sister. I'm happy to say that she

1. Billie Hawks, Jr., "Lonely Voices" *The Genesis Songbook* (Illinois: Agape, 1973)

decided that she was willing to pay the price to be her own person.

The person who lives a life based on his or her own philosophy and morals will walk to the beat of a different drummer. I was reminded of this by a conversation I had with a university professor a few years ago. He was depressed because he felt trapped in his occupation. As he talked about his life at the university, I sensed his struggling with the desire for acceptance of himself and his ideas by his peers. Yet he couldn't play along with their destructive games. His loyalty was with the students, especially those who were hurting. Years before, a policeman and a teacher had helped him put his life on a positive course, when he was floundering as a young man.

He said to me, "I'll never be like the rest of the professors in this department, because I can't compromise my principles. I'll never fit in." I admired his convictions and reminded him that the price he was paying was loneliness. He had won in the sense that he would never be like the others.

Ironically, those who do make the decision to follow the crowd, do not escape from loneliness. Loneliness has a way of following us around, even in a crowd. In fact, the crowd-pleaser feels the most painful and harmful form of loneliness: the loneliness of self-compromise. In spite of the outward signs of gaity, fun, good times and friendship, the crowd-pleaser suffers from not believing or trusting himself enough to stand up for his convictions. When faced with a compromising situation, the crowd-pleaser compromises himself.

I wonder if people are not lonelier now than ever before. The problem of loneliness is most acute among the aged. An eighty-four-year-old woman in Los Angeles asked this question of a newspaper reporter: "Isn't anybody else lonely like me?"

In a youth-oriented culture, who cares for those who are old? Yet the number of people who are making up that percentage of our population known as senior citizens is rapidly increasing each year. Since medical science has eliminated most of the diseases that killed infants and children, we now have a life expectancy change from 47 years in 1900, to 71 years in 1970. By the year 2020, 25% of our population could be over 25 years of age.

The tragic myths we have about old age have resulted in a large segment of the elderly becoming poor just because they are old. The elderly fall forgotten, alienated, useless, lonely, burdensome and undernourished. Listen to the frustrations of an older person whose doctor doesn't listen or care about his health. For most of the elderly, the fear of a lonely, incapacitating old age far outweighs the fear of death. A very provocative book to read on this subject is *Why Survive—Being Old In America,* by Dr. Robert Butler.[2]

Loneliness seems to be in the air in our contemporary society. We have become so mobile, so transient, so preoccupied with our own personal life-styles that we seldom have time for others. One of the saddest occurences of our times is the disappearance of friendship. How many close friends do you have? How many new friends have you recently cultivated? The society pages unknowingly paint revealing pictures of contemporary social life when they write glowingly about a party the "Got Rocks" had for two hundred of their intimate friends!

There is another brand of loneliness being widely marketed today. It comes wrapped in the trappings of being a "free spirit." The package is labeled "Do Your Own Thing," and its contents are: be liberated; don't make commitments like marriage; be cool; be one of the beautiful people; be free, so that no one gets hurt; just make love and move on. Loneliness is hidden behind glittery lights, a driving beat and another sip of white wine.

Clark Moustakas writes in his book, *Loneliness:*

> Why is it that so many individuals in modern life yearn for a fundamental relatedness to others, but are unable to experience it? What is it that stands between man and man? Why is it that in face to face meetings, man is unable to be spontaneous, truthful and direct with his fellow man? What makes so many people today act in opposition to their own natures, to their own desires and requirements? Why is self-estrangement and fear of loneliness so common in modern life?"[3]

One year, at the holiday season, when Jeannie and I didn't receive any invitations to all the usual festive gatherings, we began to have the uneasy feeling that something was wrong with us. We began to cautiously ask other people we knew and liked if they had received invitations. No, they hadn't either. The truth came out; we were all waiting for someone else to do the inviting. It was the "other guy's" responsibility to make the first move. We had all failed to practice the art of friendship.

Loneliness will always be a barrier until we can face our own alienation, look at our values or lack of values, find out a reason for being, and have the courage to throw away our masks and

2. Robert N. Butler, *Why Survive? Being Old In America* (New York: Harper & Row, 1975)

3. Clark E. Moustakas, *Loneliness* (New York: Prentice-Hall, Inc., 1961)

reveal what we think, feel, fear, hope and dream to another person. In John Powell's book *Why Am I Afraid to Tell You Who I Am?* are those poignant words, "Most of us feel that others will not tolerate much emotional honesty in communication. We would rather defend our dishonesty on the grounds that it might hurt others, and having rationalized our phoniness into nobility, we settle for superficial relationships."[4]

Boredom is the constant companion of loneliness. Boredom is a basic attitude toward life, rather than a person (she's so boring!) or activity (what a boring party!). This pervasive boredom becomes a lifeless desert in which nothing can grow and nothing is precious. Some of the loneliest people I have ever listened to and tried to help have been the most determined and successful in destroying every opportunity to break out of the prison of loneliness. They work hard at being lonely; they avoid friendship and intimacy. They are extremely successful at being lonely, and yet they still complain of loneliness and boredom. One fine day, I finally realized a truth about these people: they have a right to be miserable. They work hard at being miserable and at staying miserable.

As painful as loneliness can be, it can produce some of the most significant growing times in our lives. The very act of being lonely can become the impetus for personal growth and insight. *Loneliness* can create times of *aloneness*. Now there is a difference. This aloneness is quite different from the loneliness which we fear.

One of the characteristics of loneliness is that the individual is constantly reaching out to touch other people, trying to hold on to them, and yet at the same time pushing them away. He is desperately clutching at them, and this clutching *leaves him less free than ever*. He is lonely, and yet constantly bound, dependent upon other people.

Aloneness is only experienced when a person realizes that he needs to quit this desperate clutching at people, clutching at things, and even clutching at God to make himself happy and whole. To be alone means letting go in the struggle to always try to be in control of self, situations and people. When a person is alone, he is not lonely in the sense of yearning for people to make things right.

Jesus' thirty-three years here on this earth was the supreme example of the meaning of aloneness. Because his ministry was a sensational, crowd-drawing, demanding experience, he con-

4. John Powell, *Why Am I Afraid to Tell You Who I Am?* (Niles, Illinois: Argus Communications, 1969) (hereafter cited as *Why Am I Afraid to Tell You Who I Am?*)

stantly had to retreat from the crowds to seek out aloneness in order to be with God. During the crucifixion, we see him expressing the feelings of aloneness in the letting go of his mother and his disciples. They were there with him, but only he could experience what was happening on the cross. He turns the reponsibility for his mother over to John by saying, " 'Dear woman, here is your son,' and to the disciple, 'Here is your mother.' "[5]

As the crucifixion progresses, Jesus experiences the pain of ultimate aloneness: the feeling of the silence of God, the abandonment of God. He cries out, "My God, my God, why have you forsaken me?"[6] This is stark aloneness, genuine aloneness. At this point Christ says, "Father, into your hands I commit my spirit."[7] Will God riase him from the dead? He thinks so, he hopes so, he trusts so, but the only thing is to let go and let God provide the answer.

Dr. Paul Morentz, a psychiatrist and Lutheran pastor, talks about the three stages of Christian growth from a different point of view than I have ever considered. He says the first stage of conversion is the stage of activity. The business of joining a church and becoming active in the work of the church is all consuming. The active life of the Christian is very satisfying at first, but if we have volunteered, or been volunteered once too often, we discover a certain weariness with serving on a committee or heading a stewardship drive. We find ourselves becoming sacrificial victims of religious hyperactivity.

A period of questioning then begins as to whether there has been a mistake in believing that all that perspiration is the same as inspiration. The religious phrases and cliches' begin to pall, and we realize that we may know all about God, but do we know God?

"Indeed one of the greatest dangers to be avoided is to confuse words with facts: the fetishness of words prevents the understanding of reality," wrote Eric Fromm in *Beyond the Chains of Illusion.*

Fromm continues to say that "Although the vast majority of all Americans believe in God, this belief in God has very little consequence for action and the conduct of life....If there is anything to be taken seriously in our profession of God, it is to recognize the fact that God has become an idol. Not an idol of wood or stone like the ones our ancestors worshiped, but an idol of words, phrases, doctrines."[8]

5. John 19:26-27    6. Mark 15:34    7. Luke 23:46

8. Erich Fromm, *Beyond the Chains of Illusion* (New York: Pocket Books, Inc., 1963)

28

Thus, a person can enter into the second state of conversion, which is withdrawal from the activities of church life. It is a period filled with doubts, questions and a reexamination of our Christian life. It is at this time that the silence of God on these matters is deafening. The more we search for answers, the fewer answers we find. We have our beliefs, our faith in God, but now he is silent, and we are alone. The only thing that exists is that absolute aloneness. There are moments of great self-doubt, but there is no alternative to going into that aloneness. We echo Christ's words, "Father, into your hands I commit my spirit." We hope God will pick us up, that he will accept us as we are when we stop struggling against him, but we don't know that he will, because we haven't walked that way yet. We haven't been through it, and all the assurance of others who have doesn't do a bit of good. We are alone.

How long a person stays in this second stage of growth varies. A person might become very frightened and uncomfortable with the aloneness and the silence of God. He runs back to the first stage and takes up the busy church life again. He abandons his deeper spiritual quest.

When I have been at this stage of withdrawl and aloneness, it has forced me to think and experience things differently. First, I find out that my religion has gotten in the way of my knowing God. By religion, I mean the *man-made* attempts to know God, to explain him, and put him in a particular box. I have to let go of my ideas and my "religion," if I am to truly experience God.

Secondly, I find myself struggling with prayer and with what to pray for in my life. Should I pray for safety, when maybe, instead, I should be praying for faith and courage to confront a dangerous situation? Then, I am still amazed about the answers to prayer I receive! So often I say, "Lord, this is what I want, and in this manner." But in the process of waiting for an answer, I get distracted and involved in something entirely different than what I prayed about, only to be surprised again that, in this new situation, where I was not looking for God's answer, he answered my prayers. It's so hard to keep a large God in a small container; he still refuses to do things the way I believe they should be done at the time.

The last stage of growth is that of letting go, the leap of faith into the unknown, where we don't have the answers, and we don't know if God will pick us up with his hand. We are aware that something has to die within us before we can be fully alive in God; we let go and let God be God. We are still the same person, but not the same person; the direction of our lives is different. Our lives are filled with an inner glow, an inner radiance of God, like the sunlight pouring through a beautiful, stained-glass window. The leap of faith has been a leap into a lasting relationship with God.

Painfully, loneliness can help us remember our basic need of relationship. It isn't loneliness that kills us, but our reaction to loneliness. Loneliness can drive us to grow and be open, to see others as human beings with the same relationship needs. Eric Fromm writes,

> I need to be myself in order to see the other. How could I understand his fear, his sadness, his aloneness, his hope, his love, unless I feel my own fear, sadness, aloneness, hope or love? If I cannot mobilize my own human experience, mobilize it and engage myself with my fellow man, I might come to know a great deal about him, but I shall never know him. To be open is the condition to enable me to become filled with him—but I need to be I, otherwise how could I be open? I need to be myself in order to transcend the illusion of the reality of this unique self.[9]

This power of love breaks down the walls of loneliness. The decision to trust ourselves and our emotions, and to trust another by the giving of ourselves in a relationship—knowing the potential for pain, but also the potential for great gain and completion—is still a better choice than dying of loneliness.

If you want to eliminate loneliness in your life, go out and find somebody to love!

9. Ibid.

# 5

# Should I Armor-Plate My Heart?

The basic response given to primitive man when he was confronted with a dangerous situation was to respond in one of two ways: he could run from the danger, or he could stay and fight. When primitive man took a stroll through the forest primeval, and suddenly came face to face with a saber-toothed tiger, he didn't have time to think about what to do. He learned how to run, quickly! In our civilized times, when we face dangerous and threatening situations, our body sends out the same messages of "fight or flight," but our modern life has become so complex that we don't know who to fight or where to run. We just "gun" our motors, going nowhere.

Scientists have labeled our modern age as The Age of Anxiety. I think it more accurate to describe our modern times as The Age of Frustration. I think the greatest source of frustration for all of us lies in the realization that there are many forces and factors determining our way of life that are totally beyond our control.

Frustration is waiting in long lines of cars to get gasoline, when we are already late for work. Frustration is finally getting a raise, and then realizing we actually have less money to spend, because we are now in a higher tax bracket and inflation has taken its toll. Frustration is more and more forms to fill out and regulations to meet. Frustration is being newly-married and facing the grim fact that a home in the suburbs is priced out of the question. Frustration is being a stock broker who, in spite of all his expert knowledge, watches the effects of some foreign country's political and economic upheaval throw his predictions out the window. Frustration can be little things like traffic congestion, idiotic television shows, and not being able to find the mate to your sock in the morning. Frustration can be a big thing like having your dreams of retiring and traveling shattered, because retirement means poverty. Frustration can be a devastating thing like a fast-paced family life where no one has the time to listen, and frustrations come out in short tempers, family

31

fights and divorces. The home is supposed to be a place of rest and renewal, but in the Age of Frustration it can be a place of pain.

How we deal with emoticnal energy is very important to our health and to our lives. Emotions are more than just feelings. Emotions are *energy*. The mind is an energy structure. A good example of this happens when we procrastinate doing things. We experience a build-up of tension due to the unfinished task. If you are like me, when the tension of unfinished tasks becomes distressful enough, I will finally stop procrastinating and complete the tasks in order to get rid of the tension. Upon completion of the tasks, I give a sigh of relief because the tension is gone.

Medical science has given us tranquilizers to calm our jangled nerves and troubled emotions. Over 50 million prescriptions are written a year for Miltown, Equanil, Librium, Valium and the rest. Often these tranquilizers are given because the consumer demands them from his physician. Often physicians give them to their patients because it is a quick and easy treatment. Short-term symptom relief can be experienced with these tranquilizers, but there is no resolution of the emotional causes of the tension. Emotional pain is blocked from awareness and denied. After all, if your boss chews you out, you don't blow up at him, but you sit on it, turning emotions of anger and frustration inward. Feelings become armor-plated. Survival becomes the ability to not feel.

The pain and tension of emotions can be denied, but the energy generated by them is still there. In time, the body will produce physiological manifestations of the conflict. These physical manifestations then produce physical symptoms, and medical help is sought. After an examination is made and tests are run, the physician will inform the patient that there is nothing organically wrong with him. There is no germ present, no organic illness. The patient is told that the problem is functional, just "nerves," and urged to relax and take a vacation. The patient becomes frustrated, because he knows that is not the answer to his problem. He feels belittled to be told the pain is all in his head, that his illness is psychosomatic, and perhaps he should see a psychiatrist. "But Doctor," the patient pleads, "the pain is real!" If the patient becomes angry and frustrated, the next step for the doctor is to refer him to a specialist and get the "crock" or "crick" out of the office.

The recognition of the influence of the mind on the body has been slow in being recognized by the medical mind. The over-emphasis on erradicating germs, fighting disease, and developing esoteric and expensive medical technology has been responsible for the neglect in developing modalities for the vast majority of people coming to the doctor's office, suffering from the wear and tear of stress in their lives. The majority of physicians are not trained to do much for these people. Carlton Fredericks relates the time in the 1920s that Dr. Smith Ely Jeliffe proposed before the New York Academy of Medicine that emotional and mental disturbances can create physical illness. His colleagues laughed at him and mockingly suggested that he join the Christian Science Church. His widow told Carlton Fredericks that her husband died of a broken heart.[1]

In 560 B.C., the Greek philosopher Socrates wrote, "There is no illness of the body apart from the mind." Dr. Franz Alexander, in his classic work *Psychosomatic Medicine: Its Principles and Applications*, says:

> The fact that the mind rules the body is, in spite of its neglect by biology and medicine, the most fundamental fact we know about the process of life. This fact we observe continuously during all our life, from the moment we awaken every morning. Our whole life consists in carrying out voluntary movements aimed at the realization of ideas and wishes, the satisfaction of subjective feelings, such as thirst and hunger. All our emotions we express through physiological processes: sorrow, by weeping; amusement, by laughing; and shame, by blushing. All emotions are accompanied by physiological changes: fear, by palpitation of the heart; anger, by increased heart activity, elevations of blood pressure and changes in carbohydrate metabolism; despair, by a deep inspiration and expiration called sighing. All these physiological phenomenon are the result of complex muscular interactions under the influence of nervous impulses....The nervous impulses arise in certain emotional situations which, in turn, originate from our interaction with other people. The originating psychological situations can be understood only in terms of psychology as total responses of the organism to its environment.[2]

Jacobson and Gelhorn's studies on the neurophysiology of emotions have proven conclusively that chronic muscle tension affects the hypothalamus. The tiny hypothalamus gland has a major function in producing emotions. Chronic muscle tension sends a message to the hypothalamus, which produces emotions of anxiety. Conversely, deep relaxation of muscles produces

1. Carlton Fredericks, *Psycho-Nutrition* (New York: Grosset and Dunlap, 1976)

2. Franz Alexander, *Psychosomatic Medicine* (New York: W.W. Norton and Co., Inc., 1950)

reduced anxiety.[3] The limbic system of the brain is connected to the hypothalamus and serves as an important link between the emotions and the body. Elmer and Alyce Green, in *Beyond Biofeedback*, state: "The relevant point is that emotional states are reflected in, or correlated with, electrophysiological activity in the limbic system."[4]

This concept of the brain as an energy structure sending out energy throughout the body, often results in tension in the muscles and organs of a person. The body and the brain are constantly reacting to pain and tension beyond the conscious awareness of the person. For example, we are not aware that the muscles in our neck, forehead or jaw have become tense, until we are forced to recognize the tension through the message of pain.

Jacobson defines tension in terms of muscular contractions. He believes that tension prepares the body for "flight," and this preparation results in the shortening of muscle fibers. These changes in muscle fibers result in an increase of voltage, or electrical stimuli, which can be measured on an electromyograph. Jacobson points out that the total musculature of the individual becomes involved in tension and fatigue, whether awake or asleep.[5] This is why a person under too much tension and stress can awaken in the morning more exhausted than he was when he went to bed. The more emotional conflict a person experiences and subsequently struggles to deny and repress, the more the energy turns inward on the person with resultant tense muscles, tissue damage, heart attacks, high blood pressure, strokes, arthritis, ulcers, colitis, respiratory problems, migraines and cancer, to name a few.

A few years ago it was practically unheard of that emotional stress might play a role in cancer. Modern cancer investigators believe that everyone carries the cancer potential within himself. Then, if this approach is correct, it raises the interesting question of why the dormant pre-cancerous state remains dormant in many, whereas in others it changes early and rapidly. One study showed that over 95% of the people with cancer were found to be emotionally repressed. They could not express rage or fear. These same factors also correlated with heart disease and stroke.

3. Herman A Dickel, Henry H. Dixon, Sr., and Charles Timothy Dickel, *Tension Control: Tension Control in a Psychiatric Setting— Experiences of Four Decades* (Blakesburg, Virginia: University Publications, 1975) (heareafter cited as *Tension Control*)

4. Elmer and Alyce Green, *Beyond Biofeedback* (New York: Dell Publishing Co., Inc., 1977) (hereafter cited as *Beyond Biofeedback*)

5. *Tension Control*

Clinical psychologist Lawrence Le Shan has spent over twenty years in studying the personality traits of people who get cancer. His work is now being discovered. Le Shan concluded that the people who had cancer had certain characteristics in common that were not possessed by those who did not have cancer. Four factors were discovered which differentiated the cancer patients from the control group:

1) Prior to diagnosis there was a loss of a relationship.

2) There was an inability to express hostility in their own defense.

3) There were feelings of unworthiness and self-dislike.

4) Tension over a relationship with one, or both, parents existed.

Le Shan further observed that 62% of the cancer patients had a traumatic event in their childhood, compared to only 10% in the control group. This emotional disruption between the patient and parent during early childhood appeared to be one of the major factors in the psychodynamic predisposition to cancer later in life.[6]

Once, when I was conducting psychotherapy for 18 teen-age girls in a residential home setting, I was shocked to discover that most of the girls (all labeled as juvenile delinquents) had experienced a traumatic event in their childhoods, and no one had asked them about those traumas. Most of the girls had someone in their families who had either committed suicide, murder, been murdered, or died suddenly. One girl said that her father called her into his bedroom, and, as she entered the room, he pulled the trigger on a pistol and blew out his brains.

None of these girls had gone through anything close to a normal grief process. Because of an early, traumatic death or loss, the child's grief goes unresolved, and instead is acted out in anger against a life that "isn't fair." The acting out in anger is mislabeled as delinquent behavior and not recognized as unresolved anger from grief. The grief is "frozen pain."

In Stephenson and Grace's findings on cancer, problems of sexual adjustment appear to be another major factor in the emotional makeup of cancer patients, particularly in women who develop cancer of the breast or cervix:

> Prominent in this study was a dislike of sexual intercourse, amounting to an actual aversion to it, in a high proportion of the patients. The failure to achieve orgasmic satisfaction during

6. L. Le Shan, and R.E. Worthington, "Some Recurrent Life History Patterns Observed in Patients with Malignant Disease" (*Journal of Nervous and Mental Disorders,* 1956)

intercourse, the high incidence of divorce, desertion, unfaithful husbands, separations, sexual intercourse with other than the marital partner, are probable indications of poor sexual adjustment.[7]

Le Shan describes his typical cancer patient thusly:

Early in life, apparently during the first seven years, damage was done to the child's ability to relate. Often this was accentuated by a physical event, such as the loss of a parent, the death of a sibling, or something of this sort. From this experience at this time, the child learned to feel that emotional relationships brought pain and desertion. Loneliness was his doom. In the usual manner of children, this was attributed to some fault of his own rather to accidental forces. Guilt and self-condemnation were the inevitable responses. The traumatic situation or crisis had not the kind of timing and intensity which would be likely to produce obvious neurotic symptoms, or to prepare the individual for psychosis in the event of later stress. From a surface viewpoint, he managed to adjust adequately to his environment. However, the orientation that social relationships were dangerous and that there was something very much wrong with him persisted and colored his life. Little real energy was invested in relationships. His cathexes (catharsis) to other people were essentially superficial and, no matter what he achieved, his basic feelings of failure predominated. To use Kierkegaard's phrase, "he was in despair of being himself." Sometime in his development, usually in our cases in late adolescence or early adulthood, a situation arose that offered an opportunity for relating to others, a perceived chance to end the deep loneliness he felt. This possibility seemed somehow "safe." Over a period of time, a period of slow and cautious experimentation, he began to pour his energies into this channel. The feelings of isolation and lostness, the deep loneliness, were greatly but never completely erased by this relationship. A tremendous amount of psychic and unusual physical energy was poured into it. The catharsis gave a meaning to life. For a period ranging from one year to over forty, they had a meaningful existence and a channel into which to pour their energy. Sometimes it was a job with a role for which they seemed particularly well adapted and which they enjoyed. Sometimes as a spouse, a parent, or both, they found a way of life that brought them closer to satisfaction and relatedness than they had ever dreamed was possible. They still found it difficult to express or defend their own wishes, but in the interest of their group or of the relationship, they could act very strongly. For a shorter or longer period, life continued on this plane. Then the blow fell. Circumstances brought an end to the relationship; their role was lost. Job retirement was forced upon them, a spouse died, children grew up,

7. H.I. Stephenson, and W.J. Grace, "Life Stress and Cancer of the Cervix" (*Psychosomatic Medicine*, 16, 1954)

became independent and no longer needed them. The immediate reaction varies. Some made desperate efforts to find substitute relationships. They tried to obtain new jobs, to make new friends, to find a new group, only to fail. Others were crushed by the blow. From a superficial view, all continued to "adjust." They continued to function and went about their daily business, but there was no more meaning and hope to their lives. Nothing gave them real satisfaction. It seemed as though the thing that they had expected and feared all their lives—utter isolation and rejection—was now their eternal doom. The early fantasy of something being basically wrong with them, something that made them unacceptable to others, returned in force. Their energy level declined because now there was no meaningful channel for its expression and the decline was soon felt. The color and zest went out of life. At some time from six months to eight years after the crucial catharsis was lost, the first symptoms of cancer appeared in the cases we observed![8]

If cancer was dormant in the people Le Shan studied, then the triggering mechanism for the cancer to break through the body's defense system was too much stress, a loss of a loved one, despair, depression, loneliness, the loss of hope and the will to live. Elmer and Alyce Green state, "Every change in the physiological state is accompanied by an appropriate change in the mental, emotional state, conscious or unconscious, and conversely, every change in the mental, emotional state, conscious or unconscious, is accompanied by an appropriate change in the physiological state."[9] In other words, the mind, body and emotions are a *unitary* system. Affect one and you cause an effect in the other.

I'm sure by now you realize that in talking about our emotions and what they can do to our minds and bodies, I am not just suggesting that you get in touch with your emotions and learn to deal with them so that you can be a "warm and fuzzy" person! Being a warm and fuzzy person is a neat way to be, but what you do with your emotional wounds is going to reflect on the way your *body* behaves (or doesn't behave). It is a matter of good health or poor health, life or death. I have already covered how to take charge of your emotions in *The Art of Hanging Loose in an Uptight World*, but I think that it is worth repeating that "nobody makes you feel any way you don't want to feel. The truth of the matter is that you, more than anyone else in your world, determine the state of your emotions. If someone offends,

8. L. Le Shan, "An Emotional Life History Pattern Associated with Neoplastic Disease" (*Annals of the New York Academy of Sciences,* 1966)

9. *Beyond Biofeedback*

hurts or disappoints you, it's because you have given him the power to do so. When you realize that, you will become master of your emotions. Until then, you're a human yo-yo, being bounced up and down and around by the changing attitudes of others."[10] When life crumbles in on you, and people do things that are destructive to you and cause you emotional pain, remember, you may not be responsible for what happened to you, but you *are* responsible for your emotional reaction to those events. You have the responsibility of deciding what to do with pain-filled energy. Ask yourself:

> How long do I want to hurt?
> How long do I want to live with fear?
> How long do I want to be depressed?
> How much more self-pity do I want?
> When will I uncork my bottled-up emotions?
> How long do I want to wait to love and live again?

10. *The Art of Hanging Loose*

# 6

## Is Stress Killing Me?

Stress is in the air. Everyone is talking about stress causing coronaries, strokes, high blood pressure, cancer, colds, ulcers, arthritis, colitis, migraines, mental breakdowns and so on. Too much stress is killing people. Is it any wonder, then, when I asked an audience of business executives, "How many of you would like to eliminate the stress in your life?" automatically every hand went up and I got a resounding, "Yes!" Then I told them that the simplest and easiest way to eliminate stress would be to die. Needless to say, they weren't very enthusiastic about my solution to stress. Like Woody Allen, the only objection they had about death was being personally present. I told them that without stress, we would be like "rigor" waiting for "mortis." No one is able to escape from stress.

Stress is an overused term with many misconceptions. Stress is like a glass of wine. A glass of wine can be relaxing and good for us, but too much alcohol, like too much stress, can destroy us. Stress is a vital and necessary element in the life of man. Kenneth Pelletier writes:

> All living things are designed with innate stress-alarm reactions which enable them to cope effectively with their environments. Without stress, there would be very little constructive activity or positive change. Two of the most basic characteristics of life, self-preservation and procreation, would not be realized without the innate stress mechanisms of all living organisms. Life without the challenges which induce stress responses would be no life at all.[1]

Stress is the mental, emotional, hormonal, neurophysiological responses that occur in a person as a result of stress-activating stimuli. I doubt that many would disagree that our modern times are filled with more stress-inducing stimuli than any other period in human history. Bad news, depressing events, conflicts and uncertainties bombard us with an alarm-

1. Kenneth R. Pelletier, *Mind as Healer, Mind as Slayer* (New York: Dell Publishing Co., Inc., 1977)

ing intensity. Thus, our stress responses constantly answer the ringing fire alarms in our lives, and in time we experience "the rate of wear and tear within the body," to quote Hans Selye, the pioneer in research on stress.[2]

I first became interested in stress after reading Selye's book, *The Stress of Life*, which was published in 1956. Selye wanted to study the syndrome of "just being sick," and to explore whether or not there is some nonspecific defense system built into the body, a mechanism to fight off any kind of disease. "Disease is not mere surrender to disease, but also fight for health; and unless there is a fight, there is no disease....The very concept of illness presupposes a clash between forces of aggression and our defenses."[3]

Selye was fascinated by the body's adaptive reactions to stimuli; he found that whether it was good or bad stimuli, the adaptive response was the same. The changes brought about by the body's adaptive reactions was called the general adaptation syndrome. This syndrome was found to develop in three stages: the alarm reaction; the stage of resistance; and the stage of exhaustion, which can result in tissue damage.[4]

The uniqueness factor present in each situation, in each individual, makes it hard to be absolute in predicting results of challenging stimuli, such as change. For some people, the source of their psychological security is in the environment and social structure that surrounds them. The change in leaving that environment creates stressful identity problems and emotional insecurity.

This uniqueness factor was dramatically demonstrated in a study done in 1962 of a group of Italian imigrants living in Roseto, Pennsylvania. The purpose of the study was to show that cholesterol was a leading factor in the cause of coronaries. The Italian familes of Roseto had settled there as early as 1882. They had preserved their peasant dress and life-style, and, as a result, they were made fun of and snubbed by their Anglo-Saxon neighbors. They reacted by becoming an even closer-knit group, which supported the old values and peasant way of life. The medical researchers found wide-spread obesity and high cholesterol rates among the Italians of Roseto—and coronary rates less than 30% of their neighbors. Subsequently, when individuals left Roseto to move to such high-stress states like New York and New Jersey, coronary heart disease increased significantly.

2. Hans Selye, *The Stress of Life* (New York: Mc Graw Hill Book Co., Inc., 1956)

3. Ibid.    4. Ibid.

Other studies among ethnic groups have shown that in closely structured societies, where an individual's security is related to the social structure, there are significantly lower coronary rates. When such a person moves away from that society and its security, to be on his own in the good old competitive U.S.A., coronary rates increase.

There are some individuals who, on the other hand, seek out change, take risks and live in stress-inducing environments. For them, change and challenge are tonics. Security is found within the person, and not in his social environment. With these people, the goal of their lives is growth, not perfection. As long as they are meeting a challenge, they feel good inside. The goal of growth allows for mistakes. Many successful businessmen have an interesting pattern: they have gone broke one or two times. But it was not a devastating factor; they were able to pick up and go on. If their goal had been one of perfectionism, they would have been ruined with that one first mistake. It is also likely that any overresponse to the stress of that mistake would have resulted in emotional and physical problems.

What happens inside our bodies when a stress situation is present? Let's take a simplified look at the anatomy of the stress response. It begins at the mid-point of our brain, in the hypothalamus. As I mentioned earlier, the hypothalamus is connected with the brain's limbic system, which is related to emotional behavior. Through the limbic system, the hypothalamus helps to stimulate emotions such as fear, rage or intense pleasure. In directing the basic physiological changes involved in the stress response, the hypothalamus regulates the autonomic nervous system. (The word autonomic is used to indicate that these nerve cells and fibers cannot be controlled at will.) The hypothalamus activates the pituitary gland which, in turn, orders the release of chemical messengers in the form of hormones into the blood stream, which activates the rest of the endocrine system. The body's principal adaptive system in the response to stress, the autonomic nervous system, is then activated by the hypothalamus. The body has its own check and balance system in the autonomic nervous system and the hormones of the endocrine system, to keep the body from running out of control.

It should be noted that the voluntary nervous system of the body controls the muscles we consciously use, as in walking, running and throwing. The autonomic or involuntary system, such as the vascular, gastrointestinal and reproductive activities, is not normally under a person's conscious control. How-

41

ever, this is no longer always true, since techniques of the mind, which have been used by the yogis and developed in biofeedback training, are now demonstrating that people can learn to control their body's autonomic functions.

The autonomic nervous system causes much activity within the body in response to activation by the hypothalamus. Muscles begin to contract and breathing becomes deeper and faster. The heart rate rises and blood vessels constrict, raising the blood pressure and almost closing the vessels just under the skin (the cold, clammy hands effect). Facial muscles contract in expressions of strong emotions. The nostrils and throat force their passages wide open. As the blood supply moves away from certain sets of muscles, action is suspended. The stomach and the intestine halt the process of digestion, and the muscles controlling the bladder and the bowels loosen.

Even the anticipation of an event can start the stress response in the body. Every Friday, when I was playing football in high school, I would be afflicted with diarrhea in anticipation of the kickoff. One of my fellow players was called "Wee Wee" Wilmoth because he was similarly afflicted; however, his took the form of a lack of bladder control before the kickoff. I was the fullback and Wee Wee was the quarterback. Together we'd be in the locker room up to the last minute yelling, "Hey coach, don't have the kick-off yet—you got half the backfield still comin'. We'll be there." And now, finally, after all these years, I know what caused our "problems." The anticipation of the stress caused the functions of the bowel and the bladder to loosen. As soon as the kick-off took place, everything was all right. But I never will forget in college when this great big tackle didn't quite make it, and uh, oh. But you didn't dare tease *him* about it. He was too big.

Other changes in the stress response include the sharpening of the sense organs and the dilation of the eyes, even when the intensity of light does not increase. Perspiration increases and saliva and mucus decrease. The ancient Chinese must have somehow known about this decrease of saliva, for they used this fact in an old lie-detector test. They would put rice in the mouths of their suspects, and on the command to swallow, the guilty one couldn't swallow the rice. I guess he suffered from "dry rice."

The stress response of the increase of hormones from the adrenal gland is easily recognized. We get a "wired" feeling, caused by the increase of the hormones of epinephrine and norepinephrine. These hormones help elevate the heart beat and blood pressure. They send a message to the spleen to release more red corpuscles, which enables the blood to clot more quickly and the bone marrow to produce more white corpuscles. The red blood cells carry oxygen, which burns food substances in order to produce energy. The adrenals also increase the amount of fat in the blood and call for the liver to produce more glycogen to fuel the body.

The pituitary secretes two hormones that play a major role in the stress response of the endocrine system. One, TTH, the thyrotrophic hormone, stimulates the thyroid to increase the body's rate of metabolism, thereby producing more energy. The other hormone, ACTH, or adrenocorticotrophic hormone, causes the adrenals to produce some 30 other hormones that are vital in the stress response. Their concentration in the blood is often taken in a laboratory as a measure of the intensity of the stress response.

Now what happens when the body is continuously challenged and remains in a state of stress too long? The third stage in the general adaptation syndrome is reached: the body experiences exhaustion, fatigue-debt, depression and finally, tissue damage.

Selye's experiments with rats showed that when a rat was continuously challenged to react to stress, with no return to normalcy, it died. When the animal was dissected, it revealed enlarged adrenal glands, shrunken lymph nodes and thymus (key organs in the immune system) and a stomach covered with bleeding ulcers.[5]

When a person is entering the third stage of chronic stress exhaustion he is getting ready to get sick, depressed, suffer tissue damage, and possibly die. Have you ever said to yourself as you face a period of demanding tasks, "I can't afford to get sick now, until this is all over." Being true to your word, you don't get sick now, but you do when it is all over. During the period of stress, you are getting yourself ready to be sick!

I once saw a woman in therapy for depression, and I enquired as to why she thought she might be sick. She responded that she had no idea why she should be so depressed. Depression was something that had just somehow "happened" to her. In answer to a question concerning what stressful events had taken place in her life in the last six months or year, she paused to think, "Well, my husband did have a heart attack about six months ago." She added rather ruefully, "His mother moved in with us to help out. Of course, it was good that she was there because I had to have a hysterectomy after that. Then, last week our son

5. Ibid.

43

Johnny got busted for dope."

I responded to her that I felt she was quite normal. With all the stress she had been through in the past six months, she should be depressed!

I have my own warning lights when I have pushed myself too hard, for too long, and am getting ready to get sick and suffer a fatigue-debt depression. My sleep becomes troubled, and when I do get to sleep, even though I'm exhausted, I awake at 2:00 or 3:00 a.m. with my mind racing. I can feel that "wired" feeling of too much adrenalin, which certainly doesn't help me get back to sleep. When I do finally doze off, my dreams are morbid nightmares of death and calamities. When I wake up, I feel worse than when I went to bed, as if I had not rested at all. During the day, I find that my fuse is short, and I bite the heads off my family members at the slightest provocation, like being asked to pass the salt. My voice is a higher pitch, and I talk too fast and say very little. I then have long periods of silence, staring into space. Finally, my keen, analytical mind tells me, "See, you've done it again." I've gotten myself into another fatigue-debt depression, with lots of exhaustion.

Chronic stress produces a very vicious and destructive cycle within a person. The body chemistry and hormones get out of balance. Emotions of depression and anxiety produce a response in the hypothalamus that keeps the stress response active. The adrenal cortex secretes a group of hormones known as pro-inflammatory and anti-inflammatory corticoids. In mild stress, the pro-inflammatory corticoids dominate, and their action is seen by the inflammation they produce when a foreign object like a microbe enters the body. The inflammation actually walls off the invading microbe and destroys it. The liver is the body's check and balance system for the amount of corticoids in the blood, and acts to reduce their levels when necessary. But under too much stress, the liver's control mechanism is bypassed, and high levels of pro-inflammatory corticoids circulate throughout the body. The result can be tissue damage and even death.

In the general adaptation syndrome, the kidney is an essential organ. Through its elimination functions, the kidneys regulate the chemical composition and water content of the blood and tissues, thereby maintaining homeostasis. (Homeostasis is the tendency of the system to maintain internal stability.) Too many corticoids over an extended period of time can produce tissue damage to the kidneys which, in turn, leads to high blood pressure.

The pro-inflammatory corticoids can also cause tears in the walls of the arteries. The body responds by repairing these tears with a build-up of cholesterol plaque, a type of scar tissue. This plaque can cause a hardening of the arteries, which results in the heart having to pump harder to circulate the blood, further elevating the blood pressure. Advanced arteriosclerosis diminishes the supply of blood and oxygen to the heart and can lead to coronary failure.

Most of us think of arteriosclerosis as a disease of the elderly, but in 1969, the World Health Organization warned that coronary heart disease had reached enormous proportions, striking more and more at younger subjects. Dr. Arthur Kraus and Dr. Abraham Lillienfeld reported in 1959 on the abrupt rise in mortality among widows and widowers, especially in the young widowed groups. After examining data published by the National Office of Vital Statistics, they reported that: "The excess risk in the widowed under age 35, compared to the married, was greater than ten-fold for at least one of the specific age-sex groups, involving several leading causes of death, including arteriosclerotic heart disease and vascular lesions of the nervous system."[6]

Dr. Lynch comments on these findings by stating that arteriosclerosis is commonly thought of as a degenerative disease that can begin in childhood and then usually progresses at a slow rate through life, but in the light of these findings, the stress of bereavement may hasten the process that usually develops at an imperceptibly slow pace over a period of decades.[7]

Chronic stress can play havoc with the body chemistry, causing it to go out of balance. An imbalance in the blood sugar can have a very disturbing effect on a person's physical, as well as emotional, well-being. Blood sugar is very important to the body. It is the one way your body stores fuel and, since the brain must be fed, the blood sugar feeds both the brain and the nervous system directly. When the blood sugar is too low, the brain and nerves develop signs of starvation, such as fatigue, shortness of breath, dizziness, headaches, dozing off, nervous irritability and dry mouth. This list of symptoms is present in hypoglycemia, or low blood sugar.

6. Arthur S. Kraus, and Abraham M. Lillienfeld, "Some Epidemiologic Aspects of the High Mortality Rate in the Young Widowed Group" (*Journal of Chronic Diseases*, 10, 1959)

7. *The Broken Heart*

After a meal is eaten, the food is digested and broken down into small particles, which are carried by the blood stream. Some of these particles are then absorbed into the blood stream as carbohydrates and are carried to the liver. The liver takes what sugar it needs out of the blood stream and stores it as glycogen. When the blood reaches the pancreas with too much blood sugar, the pancreas releases insulin, which burns up the excess blood sugar and restores it to the proper level.

Sometimes the excess blood sugar drops down before the insulin is cut off, which results in the blood sugar dropping even further below the normal level. In the counterbalancing activities within the body, nature has provided other hormones to come and block the insulin when the blood sugar is too low. A hormone from the pituitary gland and gluecorticoid from the adrenal glands are stimulated to turn off the insulin. Gluecorticoid stimulates the liver to release stored glycogen into blood sugar, which is then released into the blood stream, until a balance is achieved.

Chronic stress causes the adrenals to run low on their corticoids, which prevents the balancing of the blood sugar and produces hypoglycemic symptoms. Be cautioned that eating refined sugar does not increase blood sugar levels, but causes an even lower blood sugar from an even greater increase in insulin.

One of the most disastrous and startling effects of chronic stress is the suppression of the immune system, which is the body's first line of defense and attack upon disease. The immune system involves the thymus gland, the lymph system and the white blood cells from the bone marrow. This is a truly amazing system. For example, let's say that attacking microbes are not destroyed or contained by the work of the pro-inflammatory corticoids. At that point, the body falls back on its last and strongest line of defense, the immune system. The thymus plays a critical role in the immune response in that it relies upon impulses from the hypothalamus, in order to initiate the immune system. Experiments have shown that if a certain area of an animal's hypothalamus is stimulated, the message sent from the hypothalamus to the thymus produces an increase in the output of antibodies. But if the same area is surgically removed, his immune reactions will be destroyed.

The immune system has uncanny powers of discernment and memory. The lymphatic system is made up of T-cells originating in the thymus, and B-cells, which are white blood cells known as lymphocytes. Somehow the B-cells recognize when disease agents and other foreign materials are present and, once having learned what they are, continue to remember and react to them anytime they reappear. These B-cells initiate the immune response, signal the T-cells, and together produce a serum which destroys the disease agent or foreign material. Then the macrophages, the garbage collectors of the immune system, come and swallow up the dead cells and dispose of them. On the other hand, if chronic stress has weakened the immune system, the mutaneous carrier cells can slip past the protective screen of the B and T-cells, and begin to grow and destroy.

A French physiologist of the 19th century named Claude Bernard believed that illnesses constantly hover about us, their seeds blown by the wind, but they do not take root in the terrain unless it is ready to receive them. For Bernard, the terrain was the human body, a collection of cells and systems that are constantly shifting, altering and adjusting to pressures from within and without.

If you find yourself constantly beset by the effects of stress in your life, if you find that stress is killing you, you need to review and write down what negative and what positive changes you have experienced in the past 6 months to a year. If you are physically sick from stress, you should recall what event in the immediate past may have been "the straw that broke the camel's back." Be sure to look for both positive and negative changes in your life, remembering that stress reactions are activated by both types of change.

An example of the negative effects of positive change on the human body was dramatically shown shortly after John Paul I was elected the Pope of the Roman Catholic Church. The election to this high office of the church produced such excitement in Pope John Paul's life that his body could not make the adjustment. He was thrilled with joy over becoming the Pope, but this "positive" change in his life produced such a stress response that he died of a heart attack.

The next step in dealing with the damaging effects of stress in your life is to write down or preferably talk to someone about how you reacted emotionally to those changes. Did you do a stiff upper lip routine? A woman, who had been very active in a Christian church movement, said that for years she operated under the subtle message that if she was such a good Christian, when trouble came she should be a shining example of heroic faith, suppressing her fears, weaknesses and emotional reactions. Her body finally rebelled against this mishandling of her

**47**

emotional reactions, and she developed migraine headaches.

Next, examine the "stress activators" at your work and in your home life. Scientifically speaking, I want you to identify what gets you so uptight that you can't "hang loose" emotionally.

Now take some time and write out your philosophy of life. A table, a chair, a knife and a fork know what they are for. What are you for? To live successfully with the stress of life, a well thought-out, personal philosophy of life is the foundation of living with stress successfully.

Finally, examine your behavior. What you believe is revealed in what you do, but what you do is not always the same as what you *say* you believe. Think about that one! The following questions are designed to help you discover your own beliefs, as revealed in your behavior:

1. What is your inner picture of yourself? Do you feel good about yourself, ashamed of yourself, comfortable about yourself?

2. How do you express your emotions, and what emotions are more easily expressed than others?

3. How did your parents react to sickness and death?

4. What do you do in your life to practice good health?

5. What behaviors do you have that are detremental to your health? What are you doing about correcting them?

6. When a tragedy takes place, what is your belief about the "why" of the tragedy, and where is God in your view of tragedy?

7. What are the ways in which you are practicing self-defeating behavior?

8. How open, loving and intimate are you in significant relationships?

9. What are your greatest fears?

10. What are you most proud of about yourself? You cannot mention children or career.

11. Write your obituary.

12. Before you die, what do you need to give yourself permission to do—to feel, to eliminate, to add to—in your life?

A person creates his own reality through his core beliefs and actions. What his reality is will determine his body's ability to handle stress. Have you given yourself the permission to *be* yourself? You have that permission. Are you willing to give it to yourself?

# 7

# Harmful and Beneficial
# Solutions to Stress

"It seems so easy to mess up my life, but so hard to get it straightened out again." This expresses the feelings of many people who seek relief from the tension, depression and exhaustion of too much stress. It seems that stress causes us to do even more stressful things, thereby creating a vicious cycle. How easy it is, if we smoke, to increase from one pack of cigarettes a day to two packs a day. The increased smoking gives us the illusion of calming the nerves, but in reality it increases irritability, raises the risks of heart disease and lung cancer. When our energy is running low, coffee intake is often increased, which over-stimulates the pancreas to release more insulin into the blood stream.

In regard to food, increased stress creates a "hurry-up-and-eat" syndrome. Instead of enjoying and relaxing with a nice evening meal after a long hard day, we inhale our food without giving ourselves a chance to savor the taste. Or we reverse the situation, making food our solace for stress; we overeat, gain weight, put more strain on our hearts, and then suffer the emotional stress of being too fat. We can also begin to skip meals, snacking inbetween with junk food, and find ourselves lacking in the vitamins and minerals the body needs for good health.

A good physical work-out on a regular basis would help flush out the system and burn up the excess adrenalin, but stress fatigue makes exercise too much of an effort.

Tranquilizers offer short term relief for the anxiety and depression caused by stress, but do not offer solutions for the underlying problem of too much stress. Sleeping pills are often taken to try to get a good night's sleep, but they do not produce the kind of renewing sleep that is needed.

Alcohol is the number one "pain killer" used to help alleviate the symptoms of stress; unfortunately, it is also the number one drug problem in the United States. There are some positive effects of alcohol used in moderation, in that it may alleviate some of the tension and stress that accumulates in our complex and hectic life-style. Most people who use alcohol never become addicted to it, even though they may drink throughout their lives. On the other side of the coin, alcohol is often used in chronic stress, not to relax, but to numb the pain and forget. This abuse of alcohol is costly to personal health, marriage, family life and productivity during working hours. It is also the number one reason for fatal traffic accidents.

Alcohol is a toxic substance for which the liver takes responsibility by metabolizing it into a less harmful substance. If the liver is overworked in the breaking down of alcohol, there is a resultant protein depletion, causing atrophy and impairment of its function.

The effects of alcohol on the vitamins and minerals in the body has been reported by Alsleben and Shute in the book, *How to Survive the New Health Catastrophies*. They found that Vitamin C is destroyed by the presence of alcohol as well as is niacin (B3), riboflavin (B2), and thiamine (B1). Important trace minerals for the heart like potassium and magnesium are lost. Other minerals such as iron and zinc are lost. In regards to the heart and blood pressure, alcohol causes blood pressure to rise and releases fatty triglycerides from the liver, which may be more important than ever in heart attacks. Alcohol also accelerates the heart beat, and blood cholesterol goes up.

Since the brain must be fed, alcohol can cause the metabolism of sugar to be out of balance by disturbing the metabolism of glucose in the body and thereby increasing the desire to drink. This can lead to hypoglycemia over time.

Long time abuse of alcohol is believed to result in the formation of a new chemical in the brain called tetrahydropapaveroline, which is a substance that resembles morphine.[1] This may explain the addictive nature of alcohol, the withdrawl reaction and the need for a morning drink, like a fix, to prevent the shakes of withdrawl.

In looking for better ways to handle and reduce stress, to return the body and mind to inner harmony, I began to research the role of vitamins and minerals. If the most damaging effect of chronic stress is the suppression of the immune system, then what vitamins and minerals could have a beneficial effect on the immune system? At this writing I fully realize that my search in this area is not finished by any means. I also have found that there is an urgent need for more research in this area of body

1. H. Rudolph Alsleben, and Wilfrid E. Shute, *How to Survive the New Health Catastrophes* (Anaheim California: Survival Publications, Inc., 1973)

chemistry. Because of the lack of research, I don't expect many in the medical profession to agree with the present findings.

Dr. Albert Szent-Gyorgi, who in 1937 was the winner of the Nobel Prize for Physiology and Medicine for his discovery of ascorbic acid (vitamin C), has written about the mechanism of the action of vitamins by comparing them to lubricants, like oil in the motor of a car. He writes:

> It is wrong to look upon a vitamin as a substance which just combats specific symptoms. Like a lubricant, the vitamin makes the normal working of your body possible. If there is not enough vitamin, the working will be disturbed, leading to all sorts of damages which may accumulate and declare themselves in an early senescense and ill health....Ascorbic acid (vitamin C) helps to keep the living machinery in good shape.[2]

Irwin Stone's book, *The Healing Factor*, provides many salient facts about the action of vitamin C within the body. Vitamin C has historically been known as the vitamin that prevents scurvy in man. Nearly all animals do not get scurvy, no matter how little vitamin C is in their food, because it is manufactured in their own bodies. In nature, only three animals—man, monkeys and guinea pigs—do not manufacture their own vitamin C, but require it in their foodstuffs. Somehow for these three animals, genetics fails to provide the inborn ability to produce vitamin C.

One of the prime functions of ascorbic acid is to maintain physiological homeostasis. This means that when stressful situations arise which cause an inbalance in the body chemistry of an animal, ascorbic acid is produced in increased quantities to reestablish the normal balance of the chemistry in the body. The amount of ascorbic acid produced by the animals helps them to survive the destructive biochemical effects of stress. If the enzyme system for producing ascorbic acid is overwhelmed by too much stress, and too little ascorbic acid is produced, then the animal dies. You will recall the effects of too much stress upon the rats in Selye's experiments. The rats died, and the autopsy revealed that adrenal glands were swollen, the thymus and lymph glands had shrunk, and acid in the stomach had produced ulcers. We humans have been genetically cheated, as we don't have this built-in ability to produce ascrobic acid in response to stress. These findings, for me, place ascorbic acid in an entirely new light. All we need do is discover how much ascorbic acid is needed to reverse the effects of stress and

2. Albert Szent-Gyorgyi, "On a Substance That Can Make Us Sick (If We Do Not Eat It)" (*Executive Health,* Vol iii, No. 9, June 1977)

strengthen our immune system.

Since ascorbic acid is a water-soluable vitamin, any form of bio-chemical stress, or physical and emotional trauma, will cause a loss of ascorbic acid in the body. Conversely, when ascorbic acid is given to the body in large doses over a period of time, the body will take the amount it needs, sending it to the appropriate organs and tissues for use, and will then excrete through the urine any excess. Thus, ascorbic acid has an amazing lack of toxicity. When the various organs and tissues are examined, it is found that ascorbic acid concentrates in organs with high metabolic activity, such as the adrenal cortex, the brain, the pituitary gland, the ovaries, the eyes and other vital tissues.

Ascorbic acid acts as the lubricating oil in the machinery of the body in that, according to Stone, "it transforms a relatively inactive sugar into a highly reactive, labile, and reversible carbohydrate derivative, which readily donates or accepts electrons from its surrounding medium. Stress is known technically as an oxidation-reduction system....On a molecular basis, the whole living process is nothing more than an orderly flow and transfer of electrons. Therefore, having an abundance of a substance like ascorbic acid present in living matter makes an orderly flow and transfer of electrons proceed with greater ease and facility."[3]

Ascorbic acid has also been shown to be a potent detoxicant which counteracts and neutralizes the harmful effects of many poisons in the body, such as mercury and arsenic. Ascorbic acid also detoxifies carbon monoxide, sulfur dioxide, and carcinogens. It is the only immediate protection we have against the effects of air pollution and smoking.

Another important function of ascorbic acid is significant in the war against cancer. In 1966, Ewan Cameron wrote the book, *Hyaluronidase and Cancer*. In this work he mentions that malignant tumors are known to produce an enzyme, hyaluronidase, which attacks the intercellular cement of the surrounding tissue, and weakens the cement to such an extent as to permit invasion of the tissues by the cancerous cell. Cameron hoped that some way might be found to strengthen the intercellular cement and the surrounding tissues, and in this way build up the natural defense mechanism of the body in order to resist attack by the malignant cells.[4]

3. Irwin Stone, *Vitamin C Against Disease* (New York: Grosset and Dunlap, 1972) (hereafter cited as *Vitamin C Against Disease*)

4. Ewan Cameron, *Hyaluronidase and Cancer* (Oxford and New York: Pergamon, 1966)

Stone writes:

> One of the most important biochemical functions of ascorbic acid in the body's chemistry is the synthesis, formation and maintenance of a protein-like substance called collagen. Collagen cannot be formed without ascorbic acid, which is absolutely essential to collagen production by the body. Collagen is the body's most important structural substance. It is the ground substance, or cement, that supports and holds the tissues and organs together. It is the substance in the bones that provides the toughness and flexibility and prevents brittleness. Without it the body would just disintegrate or dissolve away. It comprises about one-third of the body's total weight of protein and is the most extensive tissue system.[5]

Ewan Cameron saw in the New York Times an account of a speech given in 1971 by Linus Pauling concerning the ability of ascorbic acid to increase the rate of synthesis of collagen. Pauling felt that the use of large dosages of ascorbic acid would strengthen the intercellular cement by the increased synthesis of collagen fibrils.[6] Upon reading this account, Cameron decided to treat advanced cancer patients with large doses of vitamin C, about 10 grams (10,000 milligrams) per day, in November of 1971. The results were compared with 1,000 control patients who were matched in sex, age, and type of cancer. The control group was treated in the same way, except for the vitamin C, and in the same hospital. The average survival time of the vitamin C treated patient was over four times that of the control patient, with a fraction of these patients having very long survival times, over twenty times the average for the controls, and no longer showed signs of malignant disease.

It is interesting to note that one patient seemed to recover completely from cancer when treated with vitamin C, but the cancer returned when the intake of vitamin C was stopped. He again recovered completely when the treatment with vitamin C was resumed, and after three years seemed to be in excellent health.[7]

Vitamin C's positive relationship to the immune system would make it a principal means of protection against cancer and other diseases. In 1976, Yonemoto, Chretien and Fehniger

5. *Vitamin C Against Disease*

6. Linus Pauling, "On Vitamin C and Cancer" *(Executive Health,* Vol xiii, No. 4, January, 1977)

7. Ewan Cameron, and Linus Pauling, "Supplemental Ascorbate in the Supportive Treatment of Cancer: Prolongation of Survival Times in Terminal Human Cancer" *(Proceedings of the National Academy of Sciences,* U.S.A. 73, 1976)

reported that an intake of 5 or 10 grams of vitamin C greatly increases the rate of the production of white blood cells, known as lymphocytes. It is established that a high rate of lymphocyte production is associated with a favorable prognosis in cancer.[8] The level of ascorbic acid in the blood affects the number and effectiveness of the white blood cells to devour and digest invading bacteria. This is one of the reasons why a lack of ascorbic acid in the body produces a lowered resistance to infecteous diseases.

The body's immune system is attracting an ever increasing interest in the war against cancer. In the movie *Joey,* which is the story of the Heisman Trophy winner John Capaletti and his younger brother Joey's fight against leukemia, there is a striking incident concerning the power of the immune system. The ravages of leukemia had weakened and supressed Joey's immune system to the point that, when he contracted chicken pox, his body's last line of defense was to go into a coma. While he was in a coma from the chicken pox, the physician commented that Joey's leukemia was in remission. Because the immune system is like a battered boxer at times, when it received the challenge of Joey's chicken pox, it figuratively got up off the canvas to fight again. It fought against any foreign body that didn't belong there, the leukemia as well as the chicken pox.

Dr. Martin F. McKneally and a group of colleagues at Albany Medical College have used a new strategy of stimulating the immune system to combat a cancer long known to be hopelessly devastating. After surgery for lung cancer, twenty-five patients were administered a preparation of live, but weakened, tuberculosis organisms designed to stimulate the patients' immune systems. During the next twelve months not one patient died, while during the same period, nine out of twenty-five other patients not receiving the tuberculosis organisms succumbed.

"Few cancer researchers believe that once a cancer is well established, it can be conquered by immunotherapy alone. What's involved is a kind of numbers game. The immune system, when stimulated, has a certain capacity to kill cancer cells—but not when the numbers are excessive."[9]

Thus, vitamin C is a powerful weapon against stress and is invaluable to the immune system in protecting the body against

8. R.H. Yonemoto, P.B. Chretien, and T.F. Fehniger, "Enhanced Lymphocyte Blastogensis by Oral Ascorbic Acid" (*American Society of Clinical Oncollagy,* 288, 1976)

9. William Stockton, "A New Clue in the Cancer Mystery" (*The New York Times Magazine,* April 2, 1978)

disease, and in the healing process. There is still much more research to be done with vitamin C, as we unravel even further all the ways ascorbic acid is utilized by the body and brain.

What do I do to alleviate the harmful effects of stress in my own life? Besides remembering my own advice to "hang loose" emotionally and be at peace with myself, I do a number of other things. First, I take a strong vitamin and mineral supplement, plus vitamin E, vitamin C, pantothenic acid, which has been shown to be helpful with stress, and zinc, which is beneficial to the immune system. Secondly, I make sure I get a lot of exercise in order to burn up harmful excess adrenalin. I cannot jog because of an old football injury, so I ride an execer cycle about 10 miles a day at 20 miles an hour. I also practice the art of visualization, which you will find listed in the exercises in the back of this book. I have learned to rest and do nothing, and not feel guilty about it. And then of course, I play for fun. I don't make play a stressful, competitive thing. I do things that satisfy me and make me feel good. In fact, I finally gave myself permission to play a trumpet and a tenor sax! My family will guarantee that I will never play as a performer. Even the cat can't stand me. But I like it, and it's fun for me. Last but not least, I've learned to accept and love myself, and that makes it possible to give away lots of love to other people. All these things play a big role in allowing the mind and body to renew itself and return to inner harmony.

# 8

# A Holistic Approach to Healing

The term "holistic" means that the whole person is viewed as a unitary being. There is no split of mind, body and soul. If man lives, it is the whole man that lives; thus, the whole man becomes sick, the whole man is healed or the whole man dies. A holistic model is concerned with staying healthy rather than following the traditional model of medicine, which is legally defined in terms of the diagnosis and treatment of disease. I firmly believe that the best way to beat the high cost of medical care is to not get sick! The emphasis in the holistic approach is on personal responsibility for health and active participation with the health professionals in the healing processes.

The holistic model also stresses the need for understanding both your external and internal environment and its role in illness and in healing. The life-style of a person is all important in the holistic approach. Important variables are a person's love life, family life, how he enjoys work, the way he plays, relaxes, his philosophy of life, what he eats and what's "eating" him. A holistic model is far more complex because of the many variables to consider.

To give an example of the variables and complexities which must be examined in the holistic approach, a very fine dentist referred a woman to me that he was treating. This dentist had spent years in continuing his education to better equip himself to treat his patients. He was very concerned about this woman, whom he had been treating for painful headaches due to a malocclusion of her teeth and muscle spasms in her jaw, a condition known as tempromandibular joint syndrome (usually called TMJ syndrome). He had been treating her with a night guard in her mouth to relieve the muscle tension during sleep, but to no avail.

During my conversation with the dentist, he told me that this woman's husband had recently asked him a very strange question. "How does high altitude relieve TMJ headaches?" The dentist was a little startled by this, and inquired why he would ask such a question. The husband's reply was that he had taken his family to Lake Tahoe for a vacation for two weeks, and during that time his wife was free of her painful headaches. As soon as they returned to the lower altitude of Stockton, California, where they lived, her pain immediately returned. When I heard this, I asked the dentist for more information:

Q. "How long has she had the TMJ headaches?"
A. "For a year and a half."

Q. "What is her occupation?"
A. "A telephone operator, but she has been on leave from her job and on disability because of her headaches."

Q. "How many children does she have, and what are their ages?
A. "Three children, ages two, four and six." (Now these are three good stress activators for any mother.)

Q. "What is the size of their home?"
A. "Small."

Q. "What changes have taken place in the family in the last year and a half, to two years?"
A. "The husband's mother moved in with them."

Q. "What nationality is the family?"
A. "Mexican." (In the Mexican-American family social structure, the wife had been demoted. In the "pecking order" of that family, the wife would have little authority.)

Q. "Anything else happen recently in the family?"
A. "The wife is studying to become a Jehovah's Witness." (Now, the wife becoming a Jehovah's Witness in a Roman Catholic family has serious ramifications. Within the theology of the Jehovah's Witnesses' religion is the belief that the Pope of the Roman Catholic Church is the Anti-Christ. Naturally, Roman Catholics are very uncomfortable with this belief.)

It was evident that the freedom from pain for the wife was due to the fact that she was enjoying the great outdoors and a more relaxed atmosphere. Returning to the valley and the stress of her home life triggered the resumption of her headaches. At that point, we had the 64,000 dollar question; what was the wife's problem?

A holistic approach to a diagnosis in a case like this is not a simple one. It is not like finding a germ, but is rather a multi-dimensional search for many factors and for answers as to how these factors are interrelated. For example, a person might have a predisposition in his body that is the result of a genetic, or inherited, weakness. This predisposition to a particular problem may not be triggered until the accumulation of stress creates a change in mineral, vitamin or endocrine balance within the body. At this time the area of weakness becomes the focus of a change. In the case of the woman with the TMJ headaches, a genetic predisposition due to the occulusal relationship of her teeth may have been present. The constant stress activators in her life resulted in chronic tension in her jaw muscles, which then created the TMJ headache. Remember, in the anatomy of stress, that the facial muscles contract in the experiencing of strong emotions.

Another level in holistic diagnosis is to explore the possible psychological purpose of the symptoms. What is the meaning of the illness and does it have a secondary gain? What is the message in the symptoms, and for whom is the message intended?

I once had a young woman, twenty years old, who came into therapy and greeted me with this statement: "I hear you are a pretty good psychologist, and you had better be a good one, because you don't have much time to work with me. I'm on the verge of committing suicide. Do you believe me?"

She did have a way of getting to the point quickly. I told her that I believed that she was serious about committing suicide, but I could not stop her if she was determined to take her life. I also pointed out to her that in her making this appointment for therapy, she was saying, "Maybe I don't have to kill myself."

Then I asked her to tell me about her problems. To start with she said, "I am an alcoholic; I have had intercourse with a sixty-year-old man on a regular basis from the time I was twelve years old until I was sixteen; I am also a lesbian; I am in an occupation I can't stand, and my parents don't like it either. That's why I'm so depressed, I'm suicidal. Now, what are you going to do?"

I was stunned. She had enough psychopathology to keep a psychotherapist busy for years, except that I did not have that much time. In fact, I realized we had very little time to prevent her from taking her life. So I asked her to think for the next one week, before I saw her again, what was the purpose of her suicide, what was the message in her suicide, and for whom would the message be intended.

At the next appointment, she talked about how, at first, my suggestions seemed ridiculous, but then things seemed to click together as she thought about her relationship with her parents, especially her father. She felt that she could never do anything to please her parents and remembered how she hated the constant criticism and ridicule she received from them while she was growing up. As she continued to talk to me about these hurtful things, she realized how much of the pain she had blocked from her mind.

Finally, I asked her to imagine herself lying on the floor, dead from suicide. Her parents would be looking at her, their dead daughter. What would they see? "They would have to discover how messed-up your life had become, wouldn't they? So how would they find out?"

"My diary," she replied. "I even wrote in there how many times I had intercourse with that sixty-year-old man—143 times."

I agreed that she would have to keep a record of that for her parents to discover. In the diary, she would tell her parents how much she hated them and how she became a lesbian and an alcoholic. "So what is your final message to your parents in your suicide?" I asked.

"Very simple," she replied. "Look at what a mess you made of my life, because you were such terrible parents. Look what you produced!"

I told her that, yes, it certainly had taken a long time for her to produce so much psychopathology, and probably a lot of energy too. It certainly was indeed a very powerful and devastating final message to send to her parents, but there was only one thing wrong with the plan. The young woman, surprised, asked what was wrong with her plan.

In response, I stated that in human communication, the message sent is not always the message received. The sender of the message makes the faulty assumption that there is only one view of reality, his, and he thinks that surely other people share that same view. "After all, I am telling it like it is." In truth, though, there are as many different worlds of reality as there are people. "For example, you sent the message to your father, saying, 'Look how you messed up my life,' but the message he receives will be entirely different. In fact, after reading the legacy in your diary, he will probably look on your dead body and scream, 'So that's the thanks a parent gets. You work and work to make your daughter into a good person, and this is how she thanks you!'"

The young woman was stunned and she said, "You even sound like him, and you never met the man!"

After a period of prolonged silence, I said to her, "You can still go ahead and commit suicide, but now you know that all the destructive energy you will use to bring yourself to that final act won't accomplish your goals. Your parents never heard you when you were alive, and they won't hear you in your suicide. The other option you have is to let go of all your destructive energy and get on with the living of your life in a positive way."

I saw her for a few more visits, and then we agreed that she was going in the right direction. She subsequently quit the job that she didn't like, bought a house trailer, and took off for the summer to do some growing and living.

I have seen people who, when they examined the purpose of their symptoms and illnesses, have found that they unconsciously sought to resolve their conflicts through illness. The hard-driving business executive, who feels guilty or unable to admit that he wants to change his life-style to a much slower and more enjoyable pace, unconsciously looks forward to a heart attack as a means to give himself permission to make that change—if he lives through the coronary.

I once had a Roman Catholic nun in therapy for suicidal depression. She was a very charming and delightful person, even though she had been in therapy for depression and suicidal behavior for years. She had made the decision to become a nun as a young teen-ager. I asked her to tell me what the purpose was for her depression and suicidal tendencies. Why did she need to be so depressed?

As we talked, it was evident that there was a pattern to her depression. She once became very depressed and suicidal after being able to study in another country, which she enjoyed very much. I asked her if depression and suicide were the only ways she could accept her desire to leave the holy life. It surprised her, and she began to see her behavior as the only way out of the religious order without feeling guilty. I gave her permission to leave in a more healthy way, and she did.

Once during a break in a lecture called "Living With Stress Successfully," a physician, who was an internist, came up to me and said that he had always set himself up as the great physician, on call day or night, but that he had carried a deep resentment and anger inside, because he never had time to relax or go fishing—until he developed cancer in one lung. Then he was able to give himself permission to sell his private practice, work part-time in the Veterans Hospital, and take time off to go fishing and enjoy life. What a dangerous and expensive price to pay for changing a life-style!

Medical science had made marvelous strides in the control and elimination of germ-based diseases. However, this is the very reason why the holistic approach to health and healing is needed so much today. A pill is not the answer to what ails 50% to 80% of the people seeking medical attention. Yet, how many of us would be angry at our doctor if he refused to prescribe any medication, saying it would not solve our problems! It is estimated that over 52,000,000 pills are prescribed each year, and over 2,200,000 non-prescription pills are bought over the counter. Medically prescribed medication is now the 11th leading cause of death in the United States.

Another problem modern medicine faces in the effort to learn more about disease and healing is the tendency toward over-specialization. We now know more and more about less and less. In fact, if you've got a problem with the right nostril of your nose and you choose a left nostril man by mistake, he'll say, "Sorry, I can't help you, but there's a man across town who's very good with right nostrils."

It is very difficult then, to see the whole person in his environment when, for example, you have been focusing in on a cancer cell. Modern medicine, with its arsenal of advanced technological equipment, has tended to become cold and impersonal, and to see the diseased organ or a broken leg, but not the whole person. Someone has suggested that the point has been reached where the only difference between a veterinarian and a physician are the clients.

Arnold Hutschnecker tells the story of the French painter Forain, who became ill and was examined by a half-dozen specialists. The heart specialists pronounced his heart in good condition; the lung specialists declared his lungs to be fine; the kidney specialists reported that his kidneys were functioning properly, and so on, until Forain broke in: "Then gentlemen, it seems that I am dying in perfect health."[1]

The World Health Organization defines health as "a state of physical, mental and social well-being, and not merely the absence of disease or infirmity." In holistic health, positive

1. Arnold A. Hutschnecker, *The Will to Live* (New York: Cornerstone Library Publications, reprinted 1974) (hereafter cited as *The Will to Live*)

wellness, not just the absence of disease or infirmity, is the goal. Traditional medicine considers a person well if he has no symptoms and falls within the normal range in a series of diagnostic tests. Yet, a person passing those tests with flying colors one day, has been known to drop dead of a heart attack the next. The electrocardiogram had shown the heart to be normal. This "well" person might have recently experienced an increase in stress, smoked heavily, consumed too much alcohol and eaten an average amount of refined sugar in his diet (100-120 pounds a year). He was not examined for his eating habits and nutritional behavior. This "well" person might have gotten no exercise, may have been overweight, and emotionally "constipated." In the holistic view, this person was not well, but in the process of "getting ready to get sick."

Hutschnecker, in his book *The Will to Live,* writes, "But slowly, painfully, we are relearning in new ways the Hippocratic truth: if a part is ill, the whole is ill. Illness is more than a malfunctioning system or a diseased organ. Illness is the outer expression of a deep and possibly dangerous struggle going on within."[2]

2. Ibid.

# 9

## The Will to Health

Do you want to be healed? This is the most important question to be asked of a person when they are ill. It confronts the sick person with a choice. Health or sickness, life or death; which do you chose?

One of the main reasons why this question is sometimes difficult to answer with a resounding, "Yes, I want to get well. I want to live," is that we have been bombarded and programmed to view ourselves as helpless victims. We give all the responsibility for health to the doctors. When we get sick, we go to the doctor and we say, "Well, here I am, you're the doctor, cure me."

In a preventative approach, we are responsible for living our lives, for living with our emotions, for doing positive things with ourselves, so that maybe we don't need to see the physician. And if we do go and see him, it's not a "healer-healee" relationship, but rather a partnership. The old concept of the great "healer" needing a "sickee" to heal is a passive arrangement. You know the situation, you go in and say, "Well, you're the great doctor..." and he says, "Well, you're the great sickee..."

The word "patient" has become a descriptive term in a relationship where the patient has no responsibility but to be passive and wait for the doctor to perform a healing. Healing consists of a resigned waiting for a diagnosis, receiving medication and getting hospitalization, or even surgery. Have you ever tried to look at your own chart? I did that about three years ago, when I went in for a flu shot. I said to the nurse, "Let me see my chart," and she said, "You can't look at that!" and I said, "Yes, I can, our day has come. The consumer's right to know—" Then I added, "I'll tell ya' what, I won't peek at yours, if you don't peek at mine!" It was as if I was just too ignorant to understand what was going on.

Science and medicine have been placed on a pedestal as man's modern idol of worship. Is it any wonder that we feel like helpless victims of disease and have no belief that we have the power to exert a change in our bodies? If we are going to live in a world where 50% to 80% the health problems are related to the stress of life, the wear and tear in our bodies, then we must begin to take personal responsibility for our lives and our bodies.

Organized helplessness and "victimitis" is being a patient in a large hospital, surrounded by computers and electronic miracle machines, and listening to doctors making rounds with interns, talking together in complex medical terminology. The patient feels further depersonalized as he is talked *about* in this scientific "foreign" language; no one talks *to* him or takes the time to communicate to him in a simple language what is wrong, what will be done for him, and why. The question, do you want to be healed, is rather useless.

One very frustrated patient, after failing to get his physician to listen and communicate with him, said "It's like the doctor is playing 'I've Got a Secret' with my illness. Even though I have the problem, he won't tell me what it is, and I need to know."

The power of expectation according to belief is influential in determining the outcome of any situation. When a person is ill, it is easy to fall into negative attitudes and depression. Fear and anxiety are destructive emotions. These emotions become locked in our tissues. A well of tears and fears are embedded in our flesh. These emotions signal the hypothalamus to increase the stress response and suppress the immune system. A vicious downward spiral of destruction and disease insues.

Dr. O. Carl Simonton and his wife Stephanie work with cancer patients, centering their treatment in the person's attitudes toward health and cancer. We have created such a cancer phobia in our country today, that if a person hears the word "cancer" in his conscious mind, the subconscious mind responds with the word "death." The Simontons teach their cancer patients how to visualize their cancer cells being destroyed by the immune system and the chemical or radiation treatments. For the patients, this means willing and visualizing themselves well.

The Simontons became interested in biofeedback, because they felt it could better motivate their cancer patients. They were finding that 80% of the patients that came to their cancer treatment center in Fort Worth, Texas, would not try the visualization training program, because they did not believe that it was possible to change any physiological process.[1] They strongly resisted the idea that their own personalities and attitudes were in any way a part of their getting cancer, or would play an important role in their getting well again.

1. *Beyond Biofeedback*

In order to find ways to make believers out of these skeptical patients, the Simontons went to the Mennigers Institute to meet with a pioneer in biofeedback, Dr. Elmer Green. Carl Simonton felt that biofeedback would have a positive effect on the self-image of his cancer patients, as they revealed strong tendencies toward self-pity and poor self-images. Perhaps these hopeless and helpless patients could be encouraged through a demonstration of body control through biofeedback.

As a result of their meeting, the Simontons found ample evidence of the success of biofeedback. A patient, holding a thermometer in his hand and concentrating on raising the temperature, could control the reading on the thermometer. The patient's conception of his ability to influence his body was dramatically demonstrated. This example of body control changed the patient's self-image automatically.[2]

Subsequently, Carl Simonton's most significant finding in 152 cancer patients was that "a positive attitude toward treatment was a better predicator of response to treatment than was the severity of the disease. Negative beliefs can be powerful in starting any self-fulfilling prophecies of death."[3]

The will to live is what makes the difference between taping the great healing powers residing in a person or surrendering to impotence, sorrow and death. The outcome of two people, both with cancer in the same parts of their bodies, can be very different; the one survives because of a powerful will to do so, and the other, because he has surrendered to his condition, will die. Hutschnecker says, "Anxiety is one of the signs that the will to live is under attack. Depression goes a step further; it indicates a partial surrender to death."[4]

In August of 1979, my wife and I made our first trip to Europe. One of the most overpowering experiences we had was visiting the Dachau extermination camp. As we went through the museum there, we saw movies of life and death in Dachau. Coming face to face with the realities of the gas ovens and the barbed wire made me wonder how anyone wanted to survive the death camp. Many did give up and committed suicide, but for others there was the goal and the will to live beyond the camp. The power of the will to live was the difference between life and death for the survivors.

In my own experience, I have found that people are powerfully programmed by negative information and more naturally

2. Ibid.

3. O. Carl Simonton, Stephanie Matthews-Simonton, and James Creighton, *Getting Well Again* (Los Angeles: I.P. Tancher, Inc., 1978) (hereafter cited as *Getting Well Again*)

4. *The Will to Live*

develop a negative belief system about themselves and their world. Because of selective perception, we select those perceptions which match our internal beliefs. When we come across a very positive person, we tend to hold his positive ideas and beliefs with mistrust. There must be something wrong with that person.

This tendency to doubt the credibility of the positive person is illustrated in the story of the two parents who watched their son grow up with a powerful positive attitude towards everything. By the time he was five years old, his parents began to feel that there must be something wrong with him, because he was always so positive. They worried about how devastated he would be when he would finally have to face the fact that life is basically a painful, negative experience.

Finally, they decided to take their son to a psychiatrist, feeling that he could help him face the realities of life. After working to no avail with the little fellow, the psychiatrist suggested that their son be hospitalized, so that they could be more effective in breaking through his positive attitude. After a week in a psychiatric hospital, the anxious parents went to see if any progress had been made. Sadly the doctor shook his head no, and led them to a specially constructed room, filled with horse manure. As they watched their son digging through the horse manure, he looked up brightly at them and said, "With all this horse do-do around, there has to be a pony in here some place!"

The will to health means accepting personal responsibility and accountability for healing. The first step is to actively participate in discovering how you became vulnerable and sick, and then start actively involving yourself in treatment. The courageous decision to hope and to do that which promotes healing is never easy, but believing and doing the hard things in life can save your life.

In *Can You Wait Till Friday? The Psychology of Hope,* I wrote these words: "Hope is not called for in the ordinary days when life just seems to bump along on the same routine. Hope is a decision made in the darkness of life, where there is pain and despair, and often in the shadow of death...where there is hope there is life."[5]

5. Ken Olson, *Can You Wait Till Friday? The Psychology of Hope* (Phoenix, Arizona: O'Sullivan Woodside & Co., 1975) (hereafter cited as *Can You Wait Till Friday?*)

A Friend of mine once made this bold statement:
"All things are possible
to him who believes."
He didn't say all things are possible
to those who speculate,
theorize, analyze.
who are ambivalent,
skeptical,
or fearful.
to those who demand operational definitions
and quantification by measurement,
But,
"All things are possible to him who believes."

# 10

## The Healing Power of the Mind

"You can't roller skate in a buffalo herd, but you can be happy, if you've a mind to," wrote Roger Miller. We have only begun to explore the power of the mind and its power to make us happy, wealthy and healthy. Seriously, the mind is the most exciting, virtually unknown area of exploration.

In the early 1900s, a Frenchman by the name of Emile Coue' developed a therapy based on autosuggestion. His famous sentence is considered a joke: "Day by day, in every way, I am getting better and better." Coue' never claimed to cure anyone, but he taught people to cure themselves by the process of repeating this sentence over and over during a day. The only people who took him seriously were those who wanted to be healed. There is power in the repetition of words. Self-induced changes in behavior begin with an idea that, when repeated, produces emotional energy. With belief and visualization of that idea, change can be produced.

Napoleon Hill in his book, *Think and Grow Rich,* teaches people to set a goal, think about it, desire it and practice autosuggestion. He believes that "thoughts which are mixed with any of the feelings of emotions constitute a 'magnetic' force, which attracts other similar or related thoughts." Hill's famous creed is, "Whatever the mind of man can conceive and believe, it can achieve."[1] Napoleon Hill has influenced the lives of many people. Nevertheless, there is a large segment of scientific people who scoff at such simple procedures, and laugh at the idea of them ever working. Sure enough, if that is what they believe, they are right.

Years ago, I used to have so many answers, but now I don't know as much as I think I did, and I find myself having a lot more questions than answers. In the years of my pilgrimage to learn more about the power of the mind and holistic health, I have discovered that I am not as cocky as I used to be, and I have learned the wisdom of ignorance. My wisdom of ignorance helps

1. Napoleon Hill, *Think and Grow Rich* (New York: Fawcett Crest, 1960)

**68**

me keep motivated to learn and find out what works. If I do find out that I was wrong, I learn from my ignorance that I need to keep searching.

In my searching I have come across many people and ideas that have enriched my life. Maxwell Maltz, a plastic surgeon, learned how a picture in the subconscious mind could influence behavioral change. Millions have been helped by the power of the positive thinking of Dr. Norman Vincent Peale. I am even able to appreciate Mary Baker Eddy and the Christian Science religion for what it teaches about the healing power of the mind. It is a matter of keeping my mind open, realizing that not everybody is 100% right, but that I can learn something valuable from them. I can still argue with Christian Science's simplistic theology that God is everything and that God is good, therefore anything that is not good, like sickness, disease and death, don't really exist. There is an old poem that goes like this:

> *There was a faith healer from Deal,*
> *who said that pain isn't real.*
> *But when I sit on a pin,*
> *I dislike what I fancy I feel!*

The more I study, the less I know, but the more I learn, the more I am beginning to see things differently. Knowing is not the same as believing. When Carl Jung was asked toward the end of his life if he believed in a spiritual being that transcended the limits of time and space, he answered that believing was useless; it was necessary to know. Then he said, "I do not believe, I know."

William J. Bryan, Jr. in his book, *The Chosen Ones,* offers some suggestions on how the mind works, with the following rules:

1. We are not continuously reasonable people. If we were reasonable, and always acted in a reasonable fashion, we would have no need for courts or cops.

2. When predicting behavior, the conscious mind constantly lies about what the individual will is.

3. The decisions of the individual are made on a subconscious level, based on emotion rather than conscious reason.

4. All human behavior, including the decisions we make, is based on the strength of the pressure of the voltage behind past suggestions, which we have received during a lifetime of conditioning.

Bryan also believes that human behavior depends upon the number of units of mind power which are engaged by a particular suggestion. In other words, a person's behavior depends entirely upon the amount of pressure in terms of units of mind power which are behind that behavior and pushing it in that direction. If the mind is an organ of energy, then in order to increase the number of units of mind power to insure that the particular behavior is carried out, Bryan believes that one or two things, or both, must be done. First, the units of mind power must be concentrated into the stream of suggestion, so that the suggestion carries with it a great deal more power. Secondly, the suggestion must be repeated, strengthening the force or increasing the voltage by Pavlovian conditioning.[2]

In *The Art of Hanging Loose in an Uptight World,* I wrote about negative tapes.

> A negative tape, as I use the concept, refers to a habitual thought pattern in which, once the "on button" is pushed, the negative thoughts soon evoke negative emotions, which recall a series of similar bad memories from the past that go on and on, until they hypnotize you and claim power over your mind. If you've done any reading on the power of positive thinking, you know what a miraculous thing repetition can be. It convinces the subconscious, and the subconcious tells the conscious. Pretty soon your whole body is buying whatever the subconscious is selling.[3]

Alyce Green in *Beyond Biofeedback* says:

> ˙The body does not seem to care about the scientific accuracy of the command or about the results per se. It simply carries out commands. Negative, destructive commands are followed, it seems, with as much success as positive commands. It is this very fact that gives rise to the peculiar physiological behaviors called psychosomatic diseases. Patients' visualizations of success or failure, sickness or health, and ideas about their body and mind, together determine to an important extent what happens to them....The roots of psychosomatic disease lie in unconscious and involuntary domains. It is the unconcious that gets the message from oneself and from other people and the environment.[4]

One of the most difficult tasks for a person is to change the way he thinks and what he believes about himself and his world. The concept of resistance to personal change and growth by

2. William J. Bryan, Jr., *The Chosen Ones* (New York: Vantage Press, Inc., 1971) (hereafter cited as *The Chosen Ones*)

3. *The Art of Hanging Loose*    4. *Beyond Biofeedback*

people who say, " 'Sorry, but that is the way I am...I was like this in the beginning, am now, and ever shall be' is a handy motto and delusion to have around you if you don't want to grow up."[5] For some, it is a quantom step to change their reality from that of seeing themselves as helpless victims of disease, to that of accepting responsibility for becoming sick. It is even more difficult for them to believe that what is in their minds can also make them well.

One of the reasons I am fascinated by Carlos Castaneda's writings is because he is such a concrete, reasonable, logical scientist who desperately wants to learn the ways of power that Don Juan, the Indian sorcerer, possesses. In *Tales of Power*, Don Juan teaches Carlos that:

> The first act of a teacher is to introduce the idea that what we think we see is only a view, a description of the world. Every effort of a teacher is geared to prove this point to his apprentice. But accepting it seems to be one of the hardest things one can do; we are complacently caught in our particular view of the world, which compels us to feel and act as if we knew everything about the world. A teacher, from the very first act he performs, aims at stopping that view. Sorcerers call it stopping the internal dialogue, and they are convinced that it is the single most important technique that an apprentice can learn.[6]

In stopping the internal dialogue, first we must tune into and listen to what we are thinking about—brooding about—because this internal dialogue is filled with depressing, negative thoughts that will influence our body and our health. It is well known that one of the effects of depression is the slowing down of the large muscle activity. A depressed person will describe this effect as a life in slow motion, where everything is too much of an effort. Have you ever seen a depressed 100-yard dash runner? No, the picture is too incongruous.

After recognizing the internal dialogue going on in our minds, the next step is to actively interrupt this dialogue by challenging it with other thoughts. The power of the subconscious mind must be kept from activating its warehouse of negative, painful memories. One of the most effective means of dialogue interruption is the use of humor. There is a healing power in humor. In the reverse economic depression of the 30s, the need for humor produced some of the finest comics of our times. Things were so

5. *Why Am I Afraid to Tell You Who I Am?*

6. Carlos Castaneda, *Tales of Power* (New York: Simon and Schuster, 1974)

71

bad that only a good laugh could make a person feel better. The success of the television series M.A.S.H. is in the humor and laughter created by those who worked in that impossible, depressing situation. Laughter can be a sanity-saving release of tension.

In London, in the late 18th century, there lived a most humorous, entertaining clown by the name of Joseph Grimaldi. He appeared as the clown character known as Joey. According to his contemporaries, he was an incredibly funny man.

There is a story that a physician who worked with many people suffering from depression, or melancholia as they then called it, began to prescribe that they go and see the great Grimaldi. The severity of their depression determined how often a week they should go to a performance. The physician saw these patients begin to improve as a result of their laughing. As the story goes, and it sounds like a true one, one day a man appeared before the physician, saying that he was suffering from a severe case of melancholia. The physician said "Sir, you are in great luck because the great Grimaldi is in town." He then began to prescribe how many times he felt he should go and see him, when the patient interrupted him saying, "My dear doctor, I am the great Grimaldi."

I love to use humor and make people laugh, whether in psychotherapy or as a lecturer. Most people take life too seriously and forget that none of us are going to get out of this alive, so why wait to laugh, to love and to live?

Then, too, so many people's picture of God must be very fearful and morbid, because I see so few of the religious laughing. Sometimes as a guest preacher in a church, I am appalled by the lack of joy in the peoples' faces. When they sing *The Rock of Ages* they become one, and "a rock feels no pain." I believe God has a great sense of humor. If you doubt me, look in the mirror.

In hearing about the miracles of faith healing, I see God's sense of humor. Have you ever seen a faith healer praising the great faith of a person who has just been healed, only to have that person say, "But I'm an atheist!" Now, I can just see God chuckling away, because now he has this poor atheist all perplexed about his miraculous healing, and he has brought the faith healer back down to earth, trying to explain how this atheist was healed.

The most celebrated case of a recovery from a supposedly irreversible disease was documented in the *The New England Journal of Medicine* and written by the patient himself, Norman

Cousins, long-time editor of the *Saturday Review*. It is a striking account of the effective role that a positive influence can have on the subconscious mind, in healing the body.

The drama began shortly after Norman Cousins had returned from a trip to Russia where he served as a chairman of an American delegation to consider the problems of cultural exchange. It had been an exhausting trip, filled with late night meetings, paper work, ceremonial responsibilities and, on one occasion, a mix-up in plans that resulted in Cousins keeping a Soviet hostess waiting four hours for a reception that never got off the ground. During the long flight back on an overcrowded plane, Cousins began to feel an uneasiness in his bones. A week later he was hospitalized.

The diagnosis was not a very hopeful one. Dr. William Hitzig, a close friend of Cousins for more than twenty years, was candid with him about the diagnosis; the general consensus was that he was suffering from a serious collagen illness, which is a disease of the connective tissue. Since collagen is the substance which holds the tissues and organs together, Cousins was, in his own words, "becoming unstuck." In Norman Cousins' case the involvement was so extreme that he experienced great difficulty and pain in moving his joints. At the low point of his illness, his jaw was almost locked. When experts were called in, they confirmed the general opinion, adding that he also had ankylosing spondylitis, which meant that the connective tissue in the spine was disintegrating. One specialist gave him one chance in five hundred.

As Cousins reflected back on his trip to Russia, he remembered that the hotel room in which they had been staying was in a residential area. Each night a procession of diesel trucks rumbled back and forth under his open window, as there was a round-the-clock construction on a nearby housing project. Then too, the day he had left, at the airport, he had caught the exhaust of a large jet at point-blank range as it swung around on the runway. This might account for the doctors' speculation that he had also experienced heavy metal poisoning. However, Cousins' wife had been exposed also, and had suffered no adverse effects. Could it be that he was suffering from adrenal exhaustion, which would have made him less tolerable to a toxic substance?

Cousins had read Hans Selye's book, *The Stress of Life*, and remembered that Selye showed that adrenal exhaustion could be caused by emotional tension, such as frustration or supressed rage. Selye had shown how negative emotions have negative effects on the body.

Norman Cousins later wrote, "The inevitable question arose in my mind: what about the positive emotions? If negative emotions produce negative chemical changes in the body, wouldn't the positive emotions produce positive chemical changes? Is it possible that love, hope, faith, laughter, confidence and the will to live have therapeutic value? Do chemical changes occur only on the downside?"

The first step Cousins took was to find out if the aspirin and pain-killing drugs were toxic to his condition and actually harmful in the treatment of collagen illnesses. "It was unreasonable to expect positive chemical changes to take place as long as my body was being saturated with, and toxified by, pain-killing medications." He had one of his research assistants from the *Saturday Review* look up references to the drugs he was taking, to find out whether or not they could be harmful to his condition. He discovered that the aspirin he had been taking (26 per day) could have a depressing effect on the adrenals, and that the phenylbutazone (12 per day) was one of the most powerful drugs on the market, and that he was exhibiting hypersensitivity to it.

With this mind-boggling information, Cousins decided that his body would be better off without pain medication. He made the decision to live with the pain.

He further recalled reading in the medical press that vitamin C helps to oxygenate the blood, which would prove a positive factor in his case, as impaired oxygenation was a factor in collagen breakdown. He also knew that people suffering from collagen diseases are deficient in vitamin C. Could large doses of ascorbic acid combat collagen breakdown?

As Cousins discussed these ideas with Dr. Hitzig, the doctor not only listened to his patient, but told him that he admired his will to live, and that it was important that Cousins continue to believe in everything he had concluded. He was enthusiastic about working with his patient in a partnership role, and was excited about the possibilities of a recovery.

Now began an unusual course of treatment. Old movies of the Marx Brothers were brought into the hospital room. Allan Funt sent some of his "Candid Camera" films. The nurse also read many humerous books to him. Cousins made the joyous discovery that ten minutes of genuine belly laughter had an anesthetic effect and would give him at least two hours of pain-free sleep.

Next, Cousin wanted to have a slow, intravenous drip of ascorbic acid over a period of four hours. His plan was to start at 10 grams (10,000 milligrams) and then increase the dosage daily, until he reached 25 grams. Dr. Hitzig's eyes widened in disbelief over the 25 grams of ascorbic acid. He cautioned Cousins about the possibility of irritation of the veins and the potential of kidney stones. Cousins responded that he was playing for bigger stakes, and that losing some veins was not important when measured against the need to combat whatever was eating at his connective tissue.

To see if they were on the right track, sedimentation rates were tested before the treatment began, and all during the intravenous administration. Much to everyone's amazement, the sedimentation rate immediately dropped. Norman Cousins' pulse was no longer racing, his fever receeded, he was completely off drugs and was sleeping for longer hours without pain.

Next, Cousins decided that he needed to be in an atmosphere more conducive to positive emotions, so he moved out of the hospital to a hotel across the street. He was delighted to find that not only was he no longer disturbed at all hours for bed baths, temperature checks, medication dispensing, tests and examinations by hospital interns, but that the cost of the hotel room was one-third as much as the hospital.[7]

Norman Cousins did recover. The ascorbic acid played a role in both healing collagen, and as an anti-stress agent. The laughter had a healing effect because the negative emotions of illness, like fear, depression and anxiety, trigger the stress response through the limbic system and the hypothalamus. Laughter replaced the negative emotions with the positive emotions of serenity, light-heartedness and hope.

Think about it—fear can't stand to be laughed at. That's why I suggest to people whose lives are tyrannized by phobic fears to give their fears a funny name; if they can laugh at their fears, they can be in charge of them. There is healing power in the mind through laughter.

Medicine has long been intrigued with the placebo effect; i.e., giving a patient a sugar pill and seeing him improve. The only active ingredient in the pill is the power of expectation for the patient that he will get better. The doctor must also have the ability to develop a positive relationship with his patient and communicate to him positive expectations. We also know now that the placebo effect has the effect of telling the brain to produce endonphine, which reduces pain.

7. Norman Cousins, "Anatomy of an Illness: As Perceived by the Patient" (*The New England Journal of Medicine,* Vol 295, No. 26, 1976)

Research was done with two groups of patients, both with bleeding ulcers. One group was told by their physician that they were to receive a new drug that would undoubtedly produce relief. The second group was told by the nurses that a new experimental drug would be administered, but that little was known about its effects. The same drug was then given to both groups. Seventy percent of the patients in the first group showed significant improvement; the second group showed twenty-five percent significant improvement. The only difference in treatment was the positive expectancy created by the physician in the minds of the first group.

When Elmer and Alyce Green reported cases of spontaneous remissions from cancer, they discovered that these patients had used everything from a pilgrimage to Lourdes to an Arizona grapefruit cure. Whatever method they had pinned their hopes on caused a spontaneous remission. This term, "spontaneous remission," is the medical term meaning "we are ignorant of the causes of recovery." Since all the recoveries the Greens studied were related to something, what was the common factor? The only common factor was a change in the attitude of the patient to one of hope and of positive feelings.[8]

For several years I have been lecturing on living with stress successfully. To help people learn how to "stop the world" and relax, I teach them to relax their muscles and minds through visualization. It is a very easy and effective technique.

I have personally used the art of visualization very effectively for stress reduction. Once, after a period of stress, I had to start a strenuous month of promoting a new book. The day before I was to start my tour in Washington, D.C., I awoke with a sore throat and had lost my voice. I immediately began to practice visualization, seeing my white blood cells attacking the germs in my body. I also took about six grams of ascorbic acid during the day. By suppertime I was free of a sore throat and had my voice back.

The art of visualization is learning how to go from the left hemisphere of the brain to the right hemisphere. It is a process of stepping out of the conscious, logical, deductive area to the subjective, instinctive and spiritual side of our minds. In helping a group became aware that a picture in the mind can produce a physical change, I ask them to visualize a lemon in their hand. I tell them to visualize the texture of the lemon, to smell the fresh fragrance, and then to see themselves cut the lemon on a board and watch the juice run out. People immediately experience an

8. *Beyond Biofeedback*

increase of saliva in their mouths after visualizing a lemon.

It's easy to demonstrate to yourself how the power of visualization can affect the body. Close your eyes and visualize a bag filled with heavy rocks. The bag has a drawstring which is looped around your left arm. Feel the heaviness in your arm as the weight of the rocks in the bag pulls it down. Your arm is getting weaker and the bag is pulling it down and down and down. Then open your eyes and see how far your left arm has dropped. If your arm has not dropped, then I will have to tell you that you used all your visualization energy to keep that bag from pulling your arm down!

In recent years there has been a great deal of interest and research into the difference between the left and right hemispheres of the brain. The left hemisphere is involved with such activities as analytical, logical and reasoning processes, whereas the right hemisphere is involved with intuitive, subjective, emotional and psychic activities. Research has shown that men are trained more to use the left hemisphere of the brain, and women have been more involved with the subjective, emotional, intuitive right hemisphere activities. In a study of brain damage to the speech area, which is the left hemisphere, men showed significantly more impairment in verbal behavior than did women. I believe that the marked difference is due to the fact that human communication is a two-level phenomenon. The first level is the content of the message, involving the left hemisphere, but the second level of communication is the message about the content of the first message. The second level of communication involves subjective meanings and relationship aspects of conversation, which, of course, involves the right hemisphere. In the study, since the right hemisphere was not affected by brain damage, the women's verbal ability would be significantly better than that of the men.

The technique of learning the art of visualization, like any new behavior, needs to be practiced. Located in the appendix is a visualization exercise, which you will find handy to use in learning this stress-reducing technique. I'd like to share with you my personal visualization so that you will get an idea of the possibilities in store for you.

The first step is to find a "place of power" like Don Juan talked about in *Journey to Ixtlan*. Don Juan says, "It is easier to travel in dreaming when you can focus on a place of power."[9] I have learned to take pictures with my mind of beautiful places I have seen in my travels. One of my places of power is out on Puna

9. Carlos Castaneda, *Journey to Ixtlan* (New York: Simon and Schuster, 1972)

Point in Napili Bay, on Maui, Hawaii. I see myself walking into the warm and refreshing water of the blue Pacific ocean, wearing my face mask and fins. As I start swimming toward the reef, I see the sand beneath me, in the shape of little sand dunes. I hear the noise of the water caused by my swimming, and feel the increased power of the swells as I get closer to the reef. Now I see the dark shapes of the rocks and the reef, and I find my spot that allows me to swim between the rocks and reef to the other side.

On the other side of the reef, I watch the never-ending, beautiful variety of tropical fish that feed on the coral and the green neons. We say hello to each other before I continue to stretch out to swim toward Puna Point. As I go further out, the lava changes, revealing less life growing on it and fewer fish. The bottom is now sandy again, and the water deeper. My body enjoys the feeling of strength as each stroke takes me further out. Occasionally, I get a captivating look at the almost transparent goat fish. I begin to see the rocks and I feel the water change; suddenly the sea is alive with tropical fish. Soon I find a safe place to crawl out onto the rocks of Puna Point. I take off my mask, snorkell and fins and walk out onto the lava. On my right is the beauty of Fleming Beach, with its picturesque palm trees and a catamaran anchored in the bay. As I walk farther out onto the point, I see the waves sending their spray into the air. Across the channel is the lovely island of Molakai, with clouds resting on its mountain peaks. I feel the warmth of the sun as I sit down on a rock and let the water of the ocean wash over my feet. I "stop the world," relax and allow my breathing to match the harmony of the rhythm of the sea. I am at peace.

To make this technique work effectively for you, it should be practiced for at least 15 minutes a day. The ability to create pictures and see them is developed with time. A person cannot force himself to relax by saying, "I've got to relax and turn off my mind." This will produce just the opposite effect. It has the same effect of someone saying to you, "Don't think of elephants." The art of visualization is, rather, a passive "letting go" and allowing images to form in the mind. Seeing is knowing. The power of positive pictures produces a powerful change in the subconscious mind. Conversely, "a strong negative suggestion, command, or injunction in the conscious mind will produce behavior in the opposite direction by the subconscious mind."[10]

A good example of the failure of the "don't think of elephants" technique was told to me by a couple at a retreat. He was a busy

10. *The Chosen Ones*

banker who worked as a business manager for a large dental practice and needed to get away with his wife for a quiet weekend. Before they left, he gave these instructions to their 18-year-old son: "Don't take the boat out this weekend!" He further elaborated, "I don't want to check into a motel, have the phone ring and hear from the Coast Guard that you are missing in the inland waterways of North Carolina."

Predictably, just as he and his wife arrived at their hotel room for their quiet weekend, the telephone rang, and the Coast Guard informed them that their son and a friend were missing in their boat, somewhere in the inland waterways of North Carolina. They rushed back home, filled with fears for the safety of their son and puzzlement as to why he had disobeyed his father, especially after such clear instructions. It turned out that the Coast Guard had found the boys with their boat broken down in the waterways. Afterward their son said, "Truthfully, Dad, I don't know why I took the boat out."

Another example of a negative injunction having the opposite desired effect on the subconscious mind is using the word "diet" when wanting to lose weight. One time, I wanted to instruct my subconscious mind before I went out of town for a week. I had lost some weight and didn't want to gain it back, so in visualization I repeated over and over to my subconscious mind, "Cancel carbohydrates." Immediately upon leaving Phoenix, I was compelled to try every carbohydrate in sight. Only when I was returning did I realize that I had placed a negative injunction in my subconscious mind. I then reversed my tactics, visualizing positive images and words, repeating, "I can wait one second to lose weight—I will be thin, happy, young, sexy, proud—I can wait one second to lose weight..." Then I saw, in vivid color, the weight I wanted to reach. It worked!

The Simontons, in their cancer clinic in Fort Worth, teach their patients how to relax and visualize the B-cells and T-cells of the immune system attacking the cancer cells. One patient visualized the B-cells and T-cells as piranhas gobbling up the cancer cells. These patients adapt an affirmative spirit and a will to live, because of the positive support system at the clinic and within their families.

The results of this positive approach to the treatment of cancer are encouraging. In four years the Simontons treated 159 patients with diagnoses of medically incurable malignanacies. Sixty-three of the patients were still alive in 1979. The average survival time for these patients has been 24.4 months since diagnosis. Based on national norms, the life expectancy for this group is 12 months. In other words, these patients are living two times longer than patients who are receiving medical treatment alone. I highly recommend the Simontons' book, *Getting Well Again.*

The healing power of the mind has also begun to be tapped by the use of autogenic training, self-hypnosis and biofeedback. The understanding of the healing power of the mind is just beginning.

# 11

## Pain Revisited

In 1975, my wife Jeannie had an enlargement of the uterus. Fearing that it was cancer, and since it was growing at a rapidly alarming rate, the doctor performed a hysterectomy. Thankfully, it was not a cancerous growth. I felt that it would be a good idea to use hypnotism on Jeannie right after the operation, to reduce her pain and promote healing. Now Jeannie had never allowed me to use hypnotism on her, which was not an unusual reaction among spouses.

Persevering in my plans, I was in her room at the hospital when she came from the recovery room. She was still woozy from the anesthesia. Now this was my chance. She wouldn't be able to fight off my using trance-induction for the pain. So, I began to induce her into a trance. When she would grimmace from the pain, I would put my hand on her forehead and say, "The message of pain is telling your brain to relax and go deeper and deeper into drifting and dreaming. While you are drifting and dreaming, you can recall all the beautiful trips and places we have been in the world." I would then remove my hand from her forehead, and the frontalis muscles would be smooth. Then I would talk to her subconscious mind by saying, "Since the subconscious mind no longer has to pay any attention to the pain, it can direct its attention to the healing of any area in the body that needs it. The white blood cells and all that is needed to heal can work faster and faster."

I stayed with Jeannie until 10:30 p.m. that night, and every time she had a spasm of pain, I repeated the same procedure. The next morning, I asked a nurse at the nursing station how many pain shots Jeannie had requested during the night. She looked at the chart and said in an amazed tone of voice, "She requested none!"

Jeannie doesn't remember much about her stay in the hospital. She had the operation on a Saturday and was scheduled to go home the following Saturday, but on Wednesday her surgeon said, "I've never seen healing at this fast a rate. You can go home tomorrow."

Through the process of hypnosis, Jeannie's pain had been placed in a paradoxical position. Instead of causing discomfort, the message of pain worked in her mind as a message to go deeper and deeper into a hypnotic state of relaxation, and to visualize pleasant memories of our travels together. Thus, her attention was directed away from her pain, and was no longer experienced.

Dr. Ernest Hilgard in *Hypnosis in the Relief of Pain* writes about a paradox found when pain is reduced by hypnosis. "Felt pain may be reduced, while the involuntary physiological indicators of pain may persist at nearly normal levels. Does this mean that pain is registered at some level, but ignored? Is the person who is successful at reducing pain through hypnosis merely deploying his attention away from pain? Is the pain felt but immediately forgotten through some sort of amnesia process? Is the subject in an unusual state in which some subconscious part feels the pain, but the rest of him is unaware of it?"[1]

Dr. Hilgard raises many intriguing questions about pain, but he has only touched the tip of the iceberg of the problems and perplexities of pain. Pain is now a subject of study and experimentation in its own right.

There is a fundamental paradox in pain that is both helpful and harmful. Pain is beneficial in that it gives useful information when something needs to be attended to and fixed. Pain also protects from further injury until the condition, say a broken leg, has improved enough so as to prevent further injury. A friend of mine had a numb right forefinger, due to being wounded in World War II. One day, much to his dismay, while he was ironing his pants, he smelled burning flesh and looked down to discover it was his finger.

Emotional pain and tension, as I mentioned before, can be a stimulus to behavioral growth and change. Sometimes a person doesn't want to change his behavior until what he does hurts so much that he has to change to get away from too much pain and tension. Maslow said, "A satisfied need won't motivate." As long as a person is a satisfied "fat cat," he won't be motivated to change until he experiences enough stress and strain.

Sometimes, though, a pain comes too late, like in diseases that strike without the warning of pain, as is often true in the case of cancer, especially when it is not widely spread throughout the

1. Ernest R. and Josephine Hilgard, *Hypnosis in the Relief of Pain* (Los Altos, California: William Kaufman Inc., 1975)

body. This is the kind of chronic pain that serves no beneficial purpose, is destructive and often incapacitating.

For millions of people, pain is not a symptom but rather a disease in itself. Those who suffer chronic pain find that it becomes a way of life. They go from doctor to surgeon, and to anyone else who offers a glimmer of hope for relief.

Back pain alone accounts for more than 18 million office visits to physicians. Dr. C. Norman Shealy, in his book *The Pain Game*, strongly believes that there are far too many operations for low back pain, particularly when it is caused by the pressure of a bulging or degenerate disk on a nerve, rather than by a disk that has actually ruptured. Shealy reports that up to 40% of patients undergoing this back surgery fail to get relief, and often the surgery itself can cause scar tissue that only increases the pain.[2]

The financial cost of chronic pain is incalcuable. Some experts estimate the price tag at about $50 billion a year in medical bills, lost wages and workers' compensation. An article in *Newsweek* reports that the average chronic pain patient has suffered for seven years, undergone from three to five major operations and spent from $50,000 to $100,000 in doctors' bills. In-between the operations, he has taken countless drugs, from tranquilizers and muscle relaxants to potent narcotics, and there is at least a 50-50 chance that he has acquired a drug habit along the way."[3]

Nowhere has the traditional medical model been more destructive than in the programming of the chronic pain patient to be a passive, helpless victim. The people who must live with chronic pain live on an emotional rollercoaster, hoping against hope for relief from pain. They undergo personality changes that are drug-induced, and suffer from depression and irritability. Often they drink too much alcohol. They are weighed down not only with pain, but with guilt for not being better spouses, or not being able to care for themselves and their families. They are very angry and frustrated at doctors who offer no new help. As a result, their doctors respond defensively toward them or experience frustration at not being able to help. Often they end up trying to refer these "crocks" to someone else.

There is new hope for the chronic pain sufferer, in that pain clinics have been developed all over the country to try new approaches to alleviate pain. Whether it is organically or emo-

2. Dr. Norman G. Shealy, *The Pain Game* (Millbrae, California: Celestial Arts, 1976) (hereafter cited as *The Pain Game*)

3. Matt Clark, Marianna Gosnell and Dan Shapiro, "The New War on Pain" (*Newsweek*, April 25, 1977) (hereafter cited as "The New War on Pain")

tionally caused, or the result of chronic stress, pain is pain. Chronic pain is not simply a result of body damage, but is also influenced by stress, attention, suggestion, prior conditioning, religious and cultural variables, and the secondary gains of pain and illness.

By the time a chronic pain person usually reaches a pain clinic, he has received extensive programming to see himself as a helpless, hopeless, passive victim of pain. He has often surrendered to the role of sickness. He has either been told, or he himself seeks to avoid physical activities and has become dependent on drugs, physicians and a hope for some miracle to come out of the blue and relieve his pain.

Dr. Shealy states that this "pain game" is an expensive and emotionally debilitating experience both for the patient and his family, and a long-standing disappointment for the medical profession. There is no fun in this game. The pain game is learned behavior. "As long as the patient allows his suffering to govern his behavior, that is the 'game' he is playing and there is little chance for relief. As the game has traditionally been played, there are no winners."[4]

Pain is seen as more than just a hurt, but for all too many it is a life-style. Pain as a symptom says there is a serious disturbance in the body. Shealy says, "It is the reaction to pain, however, that determines whether the symptom has become a habit."[5]

I need to clarify here that the pain person needs to understand the mind-body relationship as a whole, interacting unit. His pain is not "in his head," nor is he crazy. To be told, "It's all in your head," especially if it isn't even your head that hurts, is no help. Very often the pain person is deeply depressed and filled with self-pity. The negative tape of the pain person is "The Ain't Fair Blues." Learning how to interrupt, turn off and flush away that negative tape is very important in the battle against pain. The unresolved emotional conflicts with their undissipated energy are often locked into the "armor plating" of their muscles and joints. It is vital for pain to be "demystified" by helping the pain person understand the stress activators which contribute to his pain. Real help comes with learning how to respond to those stress-activating situations that can be filled with so many destructive emotions.

One of the psychological approaches to the chronic pain person is behavior modification. Some people have "learned pain" and have been rewarded for it by their families and physicians. Some have disability compensation and are therefore rewarded

4. *The Pain Game*    5. Ibid.

for their pain, so in a sense, they cannot afford not to have pain, especially if there is a law suit pending.

These secondary gains from pain can have a disastrous effect on a marriage. The chronic pain person hurts too much to work, to enjoy sexual satisfaction, to participate in leisure time activities. He tends to seek attention by complaining, moaning, whining, limping and requiring care from another person. The resultant guilt and self-punishment creates yet another powerful reinforcer for pain.

I have found that being honest and truthful with people pays off. Even if I am blunt at times, I will vigorously attempt to break up the "games" that Eric Berne wrote about such as, "You're the Doctor," "Wooden Leg," and "Yes, But."

I once had a chronic pain person who wore out a number of physicians and psychiatrists by her determination to remain miserable and be a "sicky." My first instruction to her was to "shut up" and not talk about her pain and physical complaints at home. I noticed an envious smile creep across her husband's face when I gave her these instructions. I said that she would be surprised at how much better she would feel, and how much happier her husband would be. Sure enough, the next week she walked into the office with a positive and strong posture, sat down and reported that she felt better than she had in years. Her husband agreed.

After talking about how good she felt, she suddenly realized that she had also given up something very important to her; she was losing her role as a sick person with all those secondary gains. Instantly she changed her positive body position, and her confident voice became a whiny, "poor little me" again. I called this to her attention only to hear, "But Doctor, I still have these problems." We again tried to reestablish the therapeutic contract of personal responsibility for her life, but she refused to accept the contract, and I had to say "good-bye."

Various methods of pain control are available to the pain person: autogenics, biofeedback, hypnosis, visualization and deep muscle relaxation are used to teach the person to take control of his pain and to relax and distract attention away from the pain. The Simontons say that the fear of pain with their cancer patients is often the most frightening aspect of the disease. Every ache and pain has a new meaning.[6]

The use of visualization and muscle relaxation with cancer patients causes a reduction of tension in the body and a decrease in pain. For example, in deep relaxation a person sees himself go

6. *Getting Well Again*

over a wall and turn off the pain button. Or in visualization, it helps to give the pain a name and see it as a rather ridiculous creature that can be ordered away or reduced to the size of a tennis ball and thrown away.

The age of electronics has developed an instrument which can be implanted just under the skin, and uses a miniature radio transmitter carried outside the body. It allows those who are in severe pain to turn off the pain by blocking pain messages going up the spinal column. This instrument was specially designed to aid in persistent backache and the phantom limb pain that amputees often experience.

New advances have been made in the relief of pain for the terminally ill. The "Brompton mixture," which was named after a London hospital, is a "cocktail" of morphine, antidepressants and other drugs. It is used where life expectancy is relatively short and addiction is not a major consideration. In one study, up to 90% of cancer patients got relief from pain without undue grogginess, or the need for increased dosages.[7] There is also a revival of the old hospice movement for the dying. Getting them out of the hospital and into a home-like environment has enabled the dying to accept death with dignity, and their family members to feel more relaxed and natural.

For headache pain patients, the tension (muscle contraction) headache is relieved through deep relaxation techniques and hypnosis. For migraine or vascular headaches, a thermometer is held in the hand and is used as an aid to help the person learn to warm his hands, which alters the pattern of blood volume in the body, shifting some of the blood away from the head and causing a reduction in pain.

There is another type of headache that is often misdiagnosed or is not even recognized. The temporomandibular joint disorder, or TMJ, causes head, neck and facial pain due to malocclusion of the teeth, that is, the way the teeth fit together.

The temporomandibular joint is perhaps the most active joint in the body. It is the hinge at the side of the face that connects the jaw, or mandible, to the temporal bone of the skull. It moves every time one opens and closes the mouth. This joint can be put out of place by a blow to the jaw, a birth defect, constant clenching of the teeth, grinding the teeth at night or opening the jaw too wide. The displacement of the joint presses on the nerves and causes all kinds of head, face and neck pain.

7. "The New War on Pain"

A dentist friend of mine, Dr. Brenden Stack, classified TMJ symptoms into several groups:

1. Pre-teens—headaches and earaches. These patients are frequently sent home from school several times each week because they are in pain and can't cope with school work. Their grades are not as good as they should be and they have learning difficulties. Yet they have been checked for glasses, their ears have been checked and they have a high I.Q. etc., and no explanation can be found for their poor performances.

2. Teen-agers—popping and clicking of their joints, plus headaches and earaches. Their performance in school is also affected.

3. Twenties—all of the above symptoms, plus a grating sound in their jaw joint.

4. Thirties—all of the above symptoms, plus jaw joint pain, increasingly severe headaches, neck pain, and increasing ear sounds, such as ringing or roaring.

5. Forties—all of the above, plus arthritic degeneration of the jaw joint. Over time, the muscles in the body that have responded to compensate for the spasms in the jaw muscle can cause a tilting of the pelvis and a curviture of the spine called scoliosis.[8]

A dentist who has received post graduate training in the problems of occlusion and the TMJ chronic pain syndrome is qualified to help a person with TMJ. If a dentist has been trained in dental kinesiology, he is also able to help the person with TMJ difficulties.

About 85% of TMJ patients have too much stress in their lives, which results in muscle problems and secondary irritation of the joint. Conditions such as improperly fitting teeth, bad bites and faulty nutrition are also at fault. The symptoms usually respond to muscle relaxation through biofeedback, drugs that reduce stress, moist heat, adjustment of the bite, dental splints and dietary changes. The symptoms in the remaining 15% of patients are related to arthritis and other physical problems. Newer surgical procedures have helped many of these people.[9]

When a person enters a pain clinic, he brings along his pain medications. At times it looks as if the pain person could open his own drugstore. A plan of withdrawal from medication is begun. If a person still requires medication, he is not given it on an "as needed" basis, because it is a reinforcement for pain.

8. Ann Crawford, "The Pain in Your Head Does Exist, and You're Not Crazy After All" (*Military Living*, Vol 8, No. 11, November, 1976)

9. Lawrence K. Altman, "An Overlooked Jaw Condition is Blamed for Some Head and Neck Pains" (*The New York Times*, June 1, 1976)

Instead, medication is given on a regular schedule, on a non-pain contingency basis. After withdrawal, many people are surprised to find that they feel less pain.

At pain clinics, pain people are not allowed to talk about their complaints. They are also put on an exercise program which not only makes them feel better physically, but has a positive influence in making them feel better about themselves. Shealy says that at his pain clinic in La Crosse, Wisconsin, the people are given vitamins and minerals in supertherapeutic dosages. The body chemistry of many pain people is all out of balance, due to poor nutrition and the side effects of medication. On discharge, Shealy recommends a megavitamin with minerals, once a day. Also prescribed are Vitamin E, 400 units daily, and natural vitamin C, 1,000 milligrams daily. People are discouraged from smoking, taking caffeine through coffee, tea or cola drinks. Alcohol should be limited to two or less ounces of whisky or its equivalent per day. Living a full life is encouraged. Taking pride in doing is stressed.[10] All this means come to terms with a little pain, or learning how to live above the pain. If pain people can live an active life in a positive way, their attention can be directed away from the pain so it won't be felt.

The first step a chronic pain person must take is to realize that he must be responsible for how he lives with pain and how much pain he wants to live with, because it is up to him. His attitude and the amount of preoccupation he has with his pain will determine how much pain he experiences, and how long he wants to hurt.

10. *The Pain Game*

# 12

# Healing the Hurts of Yesterday

If you have lived a few years, you have experienced the hurts inflicted by the people and events of yesterday. The key to living a fuller, happier life is to make sure that you have permitted the healing of the hurts of yesterday to take place. Some people have been deeply hurt in the past, but they tenaciously hang on to the hurt, preventing inner healing. In fact, some people are "scab-pickers" in life; every time the hurt of yesterday is about to be repaired, they "pick the scab off," so to speak, and prevent the healing.

A person who is carrying around the hurt of yesterday is like a long-distance runner who enters a race with a ship's anchor tied around his leg. He cannot run smoothly through life, free of hindrances. He wonders why he gets weary while he runs. His anchor is the hurt of yesterday.

Could it be that people refuse to let go of the anchors of yesterday's hurts because they believe that it is their fate to be trapped by that pain? Or perhaps they think that one day, by some act of magic, they can go back to yesterday and have things turn out differently. They can "live happily ever after." Mother and Daddy will love and accept them; a loved one will not die; they will not go through a divorce after all; a second chance will be given to not make a mistake, and no guilt or regrets will be experienced. If only they can get to yesterday.

I visualize this kind of person as standing in a railway station, waiting for the train to yesterday, wondering if the train to yesterday is on track number nine, and if it's on time! This person is so preoccupied with waiting for that all-important train that he hasn't even asked the station master whether or not there is a train coming.

If you are waiting for a train to yesterday, to go back there and make things turn out differently, I have news for you. There are no trains to yesterday. There never have been, and there never will be any trains to yesterday.

One of the major steps for inner healing of the hurts of yesterday is acceptance. Acceptance doesn't have to mean that you must *like* what happened to you in your yesterday, because that would be a lie. Acceptance, for example, means that if one or both of your parents hurt you, you can accept them as they were: imperfect people who caused you pain because *they* had problems. Growth and inner healing begin with this kind of understanding.

No one has ever been changed by being told, "Oh, you shouldn't be that way." The only one who can change is you. If you try to change that other person, you may end up with tension headaches, ulcers or high blood pressure. The beginning of inner healing for the hurts of yesterday is acceptance.

The next step in achieving inner healing is to understand two types of people: "dumpers" and "dumpees." Now stay with me, I know these are highly technical, psychologically diagnostic categories. A dumper is someone who gets rid of all their problems, frustrations and assorted emotional garbage by dumping it all on another person. Now, a dumpee is *really* weird! A dumpee takes all that garbage from the dumper and says, "I've got it. Now I'll hold on to it forever." Maybe dumpees are confused and think that they are like oysters who take a piece of irritating sand and, in time, make a pearl out of it. Unfortunately, dumpees are not oysters. What they are holding on to for dear life is *garbage*. Even if you give it a French pronunciation, it still stinks.

Now remember, people have a right to be miserable, to be dumpees. If you have made the decision to be a dumpee, don't complain that life stinks, especially when you are the one who is sitting on top of the garbage dump.

How does a person know if he or she is a dumpee? Here is a very simple test. If you can recall the hour, day, month and year someone hurt you, and you remember what the weather was like, or what song was playing, then you're a dumpee.

I have noticed in married couples that the wives seem to be the dumpees. In the midst of a quarrel, the wife can list all the crimes and devastating things her husband has done to her, even way back when they were first married. Hearing all this, the husband is totally bewildered. When he says that he doesn't remember all those things, his wife gets madder than ever. What the wife doesn't realize is that her husband doesn't remember any of these things, because he dumped all that garbage on her years ago and his energy to remember is gone.

90

Now, if you realize that you are a dumpee, and are tired of carrying around all that garbage, the solution is very simple. Flush it. Take all that negative energy, visualize yourself walking over to an old-fashioned toilet with the water closet up above, pull the chain and hear the sound of the flushing. You can even choose to have a funeral for your garbage and bury it. Bury it deep, cover it up, and don't go back out there periodically and dig it up to see if it's still there.

The apostle Paul wrote these powerful words for living, "Be angry, but do not sin, do not let the sun go down on your anger."[1] Paul did not say don't be angry, or don't show your anger or bottle it up. No! Be angry, but don't be destructive with your anger. Get rid of the irritations that cause anger, and solve the problems *now*. Don't let the sun go down on your anger. Paul is calling for emotional honesty. When unresolved conflict and emotional energy are kept inside for too many days, the anger becomes depression. If you think that you don't feel angry very often, remember that depression is anger turned inward.

Bitterness, resentments and hate are parasites of the mind and body and are very difficult to dislodge. These emotions block healing emotionally and physically. They are emotional cancers; they can literally eat a person up and destroy him. I think some people can't let go of these emotions because they want to have the last word or strike the last blow. Until that happens, their cancerous emotions strike a hefty blow at them.

I've been hurt once or twice in life. I have also made some very basic decisions about those events of pain. If someone has hurt me once, that is enough. I have decided that I will not hold "open house" for that person to enter my emotional life again. I am not going to hurt some more by brooding over what that person did to me. If I allow bitterness, resentment or hate to enter my life, then I must take the responsibility for pain. If I dwell on the painful event, that other person hurts me again, with my permission. No. I have decided once is enough. I will not open the door to the enemy and say, "Come on in and hurt me again."

It's true, people can be a pain, and the people that hurt us are not always from the yesterdays of our lives, but rather those who hurt us just yesterday and will probably do something to hurt us tomorrow or the next day. If you have to face a person who has recently hurt you, I would like to suggest that you use the art of visualization. Let's say that this person is a very pompous, arrogant and intimidating man. An appropriate visualization would be to see him standing before you, dressed in nothing but

1. Ephesians 4:26

**91**

a jock strap. His big, hairy belly is hanging over his jock strap, and he is wearing a silly New Year's Eve hat on his head. If the person is a woman with the same endearing qualities, you could visualize her as standing before you, having put on enough weight to be the size of a blimp, and dressed in one of those old-fashioned corsets, with all its strings about to pop.

Once in a couples' siminar which was exploring personal programming of the past, a wife responded to the question, "What was your earliest painful memory?" by saying that when she was five years old, her mother died. I inquired if she had cried a lot.

She answered by saying, "I can't remember too much about how I felt. I must have blocked it out."

When asked what happened after that, she said that she had lived with her aunt and uncle until they died suddenly, and then she had lived with her father until he died suddenly.

I asked her if she ever felt that she was jinxed, and she said, "Only in the sense that I knew that I could die at the same age my mother did. My mother died as a very young woman. When I reached that same age, it was a very rough year for me."

Then I inquired if she would like to write her mother a letter that night and tell her about all the things that had happened to her since she was five. She agreed that it would be a good idea. I then said, "You have permission to cry all those tears that are welled up inside for all those people who have died in your life."

The next day she came to the seminar with a new sparkle in her eyes and reported, "I wrote that letter to my mom and told her how I missed her and what has happened in my life. Then I cried and cried. It was such a welcome release and relief."

A day later, I taught the group the art of visualization for deep relaxation and change. This same woman came outside after the meeting and said to me, "Do you know what I visualized? I saw a little girl running through a mountain meadow, filled with wild flowers and tall grass. That little girl was so happy and free. That little girl was me!

"After the visualization, I remembered how, when I was growing up, well-meaning relatives and adults who knew about all the loved ones who had died in my life used to say to me, 'What a sad little girl.' They programmed me to be a sad little girl. No wonder I didn't know how to have fun and play. I was always to be a 'sad little girl.' But now I'm free to be happy and I can laugh and have fun."

You may be wondering why I feel I have the right to give a person permission to cry. Sometimes a person needs permission to cry or release other feelings that have been bottled-up inside for a long time. Perhaps no one has ever given you permission to cry, to feel what you need to feel, to get rid of all that energy that needs to be released. To have permission depends not upon the healing power I possess, but upon your need to hear the releasing words, "you have permission." I give you permission to allow the healings of the hurts of yesterday—NOW.

# 13

## The Enemy Who Must Be Loved

The most important factor in healing, in being healthy and living a vibrant life, is the acceptance of ourselves as being human. If we could love ourselves as we are, if we could look into the mirror and accept the good and the bad—the whole cupcake—I firmly believe that most of the hospitals would be close to empty, and the major pharmaceutical companies would be bankrupt. The research of both Le Shan and the Simontons show that a poor self-image is a major factor in people who develop cancer. I believe, as do others, that a healthy, functioning, whole person—body and mind—is dependent on a healthy self-image.

How often psychology books say, "accept and love yourself." But it seems so easy to say and so hard to do. Carl Jung wrote these powerful words in *Modern Man in Search of a Soul*:

> Perhaps this sounds very simple, but simple things are always the most difficult. In actual life it requires the greatest discipline to be simple, and the acceptance of oneself is the essence of the moral problem and the epitome of a whole outlook upon life. That I feed the hungry, that I forgive an insult, that I love my enemy in the name of Christ—all these are undoubtedly great virtues. What I do unto the least of my brethren, that I do unto Christ. But what if I should discover that the least amongst them all, the poorest of all the beggars, the most impudent of all the offenders, the very enemy himself, that these are within me, and that I myself am the enemy who must be loved—what then? As a rule, the Christian's attitude is then reversed; there is no longer any question of love or long-suffering; we say to the brother within us, "Raca" (fool), and condemn and rage against ourselves. We hide it from the world; we refuse to admit even having met this lease among the lowly in ourselves.[1]

What a powerful realization that "I myself am the enemy who must be loved."

1. Carl G. Jung, *Modern Man in Search of a Soul* (New York: Harcourt, Brace and Co., 1933) (hereafter cited as *Modern Man in Search of a Soul*)

Discovering the darker side of our being is frightening; so much effort has been used to hide this knowledge from ourselves and from the world. It is our secret. A secret, destructive energy that seldom finds release.

Recently I received a letter from a friend of ours, who was learning the freedom that self-knowledge gives. She wrote:

> The past few weeks have been like climbing out of a muddy hole. Today it feels good to be sitting on the outside, with the sun shining. Then, it is another thing to realize that I'm the one that got myself all muddy, and if I'd ever stopped a minute and turned around, I would have realized that there was a ladder there all the time. But I was too afraid to turn around! Anyway, one message I kept hearing was, "If everybody knew who I really was, and what I really think, they'd be disappointed." I'm still working on that one.
>
> I decided that I could be a good mother, and it is O.K. not to be "Super Mom." I'm not a peace-maker! Love is not based on how much I do in order to live. I've got to learn to like myself better. An old message came back, "You are only worth something when you are having babies." That's been a hard one to get rid of!

I wrote her back, and the main thing I said was, "If everybody knew who you really were, and what you really think, they would not be disappointed but relieved, because you're human too!"

One of the most difficult tasks for inner-healing is to come to grips with that certain "funny feeling" we all have about ourselves. This funny feeling is often found in an exaggerated sense in adopted children, or even more so with children who have lived in one foster home after another.

I remember one discussion with a group of these children who, each in their own way, tried to describe that certain "funny feeling" they had about themselves. One talked about a recurring dream where he would see a mother with no facial features. Another said, "Just before falling to sleep, I hear a woman's voice call me by my name, and it's a voice I've never heard before." Then the discussion began to center around about how nobody liked them, and finally, how being loved made them feel nervous and uneasy. One said, "I always feel like I have to keep testing my adopted parents to see if they really do love me." And another, "Even though my parents say, 'Look, we love you. We chose you,' it doesn't help get rid of that funny feeling."

This funny feeling they were trying to describe is born out of the puzzle as to why a parent would give a new-born child away.

Parents normally love a child at birth. "Children are expert observers, but make many mistakes in interpreting what they observe. They often draw wrong conclusions and choose mistaken ways in which to find their place," wrote Rudolph Dreikurs in *Children: The Challenge*.[2]

An adoptive child makes a wrong decision in trying to solve the puzzle, and concludes that he was given away because his parents took a look at him at birth and saw that he was a "bad seed." This faulty conclusion was not based on the feeling of having done something bad, but on the decision that "I'm bad—I am the crime." Therefore, to protect others from getting too close and finding out the secret of that certain funny feeling, he does things to keep people at a safe distance.

Another way of looking at the situation that is very close to the truth is to explain to the child, "Your mother did not give you away because you were a bad seed; quite the contrary, it was out of her love for you that she made the painful decision to give you a chance in life by giving you to a couple who could provide far more security than she could give. So it was out of your mother's love that she gave you a more secure life, with lots of love from the people who chose you to be their child.

That funny feeling is also found in children who are sensitive about their parents' happiness and somehow feel responsible for saving the marriage. There are also some children who get a non-verbal message that they were not wanted at birth. This feeling that "I'm no good" is a powerful contaminator of a self-image that is carried into adult life. One man lived with depression for years before he was able to see that he had been programmed to be responsible for his parents' life. He received a message from his father that "you only get one mistake in life." When he went to school, his mother told him, "Don't be surprised if no one likes you. Your parents have to like you. When you come home from school, don't be surprised if your mother has committed suicide." He remembered running home from school each day to see if Mother had committed suicide. Sometimes his mother would not be easily found, and he would frantically search the house to see if she had hung herself in the basement or drowned herself in the bath tub.

Further complicating this man's identity, his father had told him repeatedly, "Never trust anyone." When he told his father that he wanted to leave home to go around the world with a friend, his father told him, "If you go, you'd better never come back."

2. Rudolph Dreikurs, *Children: The Challenge* (New York: Hawthorn Books Inc., 1964)

Suicide had been in this family for years, as his grandfather had committed suicide and was denied a church burial. Eventually, his own father did commit suicide.

When this man was finally able to separate in his mind that his parents had problems that were not his problems, and that he was not responsible for their happiness or their way of life, he was able to decontaminate himself from guilt. He was finally able to come alive, and trust and love himself. Parents can be wrong. He was not a failure, he could make more than one mistake, and it was O.K. to wear a happy face.

I wonder what happens to so many of us in this business of growing up in life? Why is it such a fight? Why do so many of us feel so lousy about ourselves? It might begin when a child realizes that it is necessary and yet impossible to please his parents. It doesn't seem to be enough for a child to just develop his own uniqueness for, as parents, we have preconceived ideas of what and who the child shall be.

Often a father wants his son to follow in his footsteps. My own dad was a very talented and gifted violinist. He had a gift for music as well as a fine ear; at fourteen, he was the first violinist in the Omaha Symphony Orchestra. Then George, his first son, came along. Soon my Dad discovered that things don't always work out with your children the way you want them to. One of my earliest memories is of going to a music recital to hear my older brother play the violin in a music group. He was the only one who had a mute on his violin. He was so bad! Literally tone deaf. To this day, when you stand next to him to sing in church, every hymn sounds like "The Red River Valley."

Sometimes as parents we blow it even when a child does a great job at something. A friend of mine told me that his son was a tremendous athlete. He was, according to his father, probably the best quarterback in the state. One night, after an exciting game in which his son had thrown three touchdown passes and literally won the game, his father was complimenting him on his performance. He told him that he had played a great game, but if he had just done this one thing differently—whereupon his son interrupted him, and looking down at him from his six-foot-three frame, said, "Can't you even just say I did something good, without spoiling it?" He apologized to his son and said, "I'll try to think before I put my foot in my mouth—next time."

The highly competitive programming in our society often makes a wreck out of so many of us. Some of us think that the competitive way is *the* American Way. Where does it start?

When we are very young, we begin to collect the brownie points of life to prove ourselves. Then we go on to get educated in a system where we are given stars, ribbons and grades; we are ranked into various groups, given I.Q. scores and achievement tests. After school activities are filled with Pop Warner football, soccer, tennis lessons, competitive swimming, little leagues, lessons, lessons and more lessons. This all happens before we even become teen-agers! Approval only comes in winning, and sometimes that approval is only momentary; there is another test, another game, another contest, and we do it all over again.

What is the cost in psychological implications? No one knows. There are those who quit trying. They just get tired of losing. In competing with others, with the measuring stick being the comparison game, they fail to develop a "wonder of themselves"; they fail to grow into their own uniqueness.

Then there is a group of people who go through the motions of competing, but their creed is "I'll stay in the middle of the pack, so I won't be noticed." This way they don't have to put out much effort; they have no big dreams, but they have no big letdowns either. Just a dull, grey existence.

The system of competition does produce winners. Yes, there are many highly successful competitors in business and professional life. They wear the ribbons of success: nice homes, nice cars, nice clothes—and coronaries. Yet, heart specialists tell us that coronaries are 100% preventable.

In 1978, I had the privilege of sharing a day's lecture with Dr. Meyer Friedman in Portland Oregon. We lectured on the stress-life and coronaries. Dr. Friedman co-authored the book with Dr. Ray Rosenman entitled, *Type A Behavior and Your Heart.*

Dr. Friedman has already had his coronary, so he speaks from personal experience. He said that the first area of research into heart disease was focused on the relationship of cholesterol to heart disease. However, their studies took on an entirely different approach when one day a president of a Junior League told him that it wasn't cholesterol that was killing husbands—it was stress. Deciding that this was worth looking into, Friedman and Rosenman developed questionaires to see how people in industry ranked the various stress factors in their work. Listed were standard risks, such as dirt, smoking, anxiety, excessive competition and stress to make deadlines. More than 70% of the people picked excessive competition and the stress of making deadlines as the most stressful factors in their work.[3]

What about cholesterol? Actually, we only receive about 10%

3. Meyer Friedman and Ray Roseman, *Type A Behavior and Your Heart* (New York: Fawcett Crest, 1974)

of our cholesterol from what we eat. Ninety percent of it is manufactured within our body. A lot of cholesterol is comes from all the refined sugars and white starches that we eat, but the stress response has a direct correlation on our cholesterol levels. If we took a look at tax accountants before April 15th, gave them low cholesterol diets and then measured their cholesterol levels on April 13th, well, they'd be peaking off the paper! Then, if we took the same people, same occupation, same diet and measured their levels in June, the cholesterol would be down—flat normal.

Dr. Friedman describes the personality profiles of the men and women who are most likely to get heart attacks. The Type A personality has an intense competitive drive to get things done. He is impatient while waiting in line, waiting in traffic, or waiting for a table. The Type A will often interrupt a conversation because he can't wait for the other person to finish his sentence. Dr. Friedman once asked an interpreter why he always broke in on the conversation so abruptly. He answered, "I am afraid if I didn't say what I had on my mind then, I might forget by the time the other person finished." Dr. Friedman, in his mellowed way, softly told the man that if what he was about to say could be forgotten so quickly, maybe it wasn't worth saying at all.[4]

A Type A is the kind of person who lives life by the numbers. If he does break down and take a vacation, he finds he feels guilty because he is not working, so he rushes through his vacation. A typical Type A vacation is illustrated by the man who took his family on a two-week trip where they traveled 3,942 miles, drove through fifteen states, took 412 slides and even made it out to the Grand Canyon in Arizona. When they got to the canyon he dashed out of the car to take pictures. One of his children wanted to get out of the car and *look* at the Grand Canyon, but he told the child that they didn't have time, and besides, he could look at the pictures after they got home!

Friedman says that the Type A personality engages in polyphasic behavior; that is, doing two things at once to save time. Like brushing his teeth while taking a shower. The Type A cannot let go and relax. He is engaged in the grind of life. The basic psychological problem of the Type A personality is a lack of self-acceptance, and a lack of trusting and loving himself. Life is a contest to the end, even if it is a premature end.

The Type B personality is able to hang loose emotionally. He loves and accepts himself, and this is the source of his self-assurance and confidence. He is not striving for other people's

4. Ibid.

approval. He is able to work but to also let go of his work. He is more interested in the quality of his life. There is no necessity to always be first, to rush to make decisions and get things done. He is able to delegate responsibilities, and he takes the time to think and to be interested in areas that are not work related. He is creative and productive.[5]

When we take a look at our behavior, can we change? The first thing we have to do is to ask ourselves, do we want to change? Do we believe in change? Probably one of the hardest things in taking a look at life-styles and stress phenomenon is to keep the mind open for the possibilities of more variables than we ever thought of before, and not to close our minds and revert to tunnel vision. It's so secure to have tunnel vision. Sometimes people's minds are like concrete, thoroughly mixed-up and firmly set.

Would you like to feel good about yourself? Comfortable with who you are? The first step is to stop being so critical of yourself. Stop putting yourself down and then slowly dying of self-pity. Carl Jung was right. You yourself are the enemy who must be loved.

I was once talking with a group of high school teachers and school personnel about the negative attitudes that so many teen-agers have and how critical a teen-ager is of himself, when a teacher spoke up and related a very stressful situation she had just observed. A number of teen-agers were teasing a fourteen-year-old freshman girl, calling her all kinds of dirty names. The girl who was being ridiculed turned on her tormenters, and with tears in her eyes, said, "You guys are real amateur dirty-name-callers. You should listen to an expert cut me down sometime. You should hear the names I call myself."

It is so easy to be critical of ourselves, to feel we will never measure up, never be good enough. But to whom must we measure up? How good must we be, before we are accepted? Are we to be a carbon copy of someone else? How can we be, when even our thumb print is a statement of our individual uniqueness?

Is it God who is demanding that we be perfect before we will be good enough to be accepted by him? According to what God says, I am accepted and loved by him on the basis that I'm not now, nor ever will be, perfect enough or good enough. I experience this love of God on the basis of my need to be loved and forgiven. This, to me, is acceptance. Acceptance of my need to be accepted! Loved because I need it so much. So I can quit trying to upstage God and give myself permission to love and accept myself.

5. Ibid.

In my book, *Hey Man! Open Up and Live,* I wrote about how a person struggles to have his ticket of self-worth and self-approval "punched." We go around looking for other people to punch our tickets. In truth, "only you can punch your own ticket. Only you can love yourself, forgive yourself, andd accept yourself just as you are. Then you'll be able to love other people and make them feel 'for real.' Punch your own ticket. Try it, you'll like it."[6]

*I Have Permission*
*I have permission to break the chains*
*of yesterday's pain.*
*After all the strife,*
*a new lease on life.*
*I have permission at last*
*to be free,*
*to be me.*
*To throw away all the masks*
*and stop those boring tasks.*
*I have permission*
*to trust,*
*to accept,*
*to love me.*
*I have permission to be the me*
       *I was meant to be.*
*It's so strange how long it took*
          *to look at me.*
*I'm not perfect,*
       *but I'm not bad.*
*I can be sad,*
       *mad,*
       *glad.*
          *laugh and love.*
*Look out, world!*
*Since I have permission to love me,*
*there's so much love to give away.*
*My love of self and others*
       *is here to stay.*

6. Ken Olson, *Hey Man! Open Up and Live* (New York: Fawcett Gold Medal, 1978)

# 14

## Spiritual Healing

I approach the area of spiritual healing with a certain amount of unsureness about my ability to handle the subject adequately. However, a book on pain and holistic healing would be incomplete without an exploration into spiritual healing.

Carl Jung criticized Freud and Adler for being one-sided, basing everything on man's physical drives. He said, "The kind of psychology they represent leaves out the psyche, and is suited to people who believe that they have no spiritual needs or aspirations. Because of their exclusive concern with drives, they still fail to satisfy the deeper spiritual needs of the patient....In a word, they do not give meaning enough to life. And it is only the meaningful that sets us free."[1]

I have found that in the main line Christian churches there is an adversion to talking about spiritual healing. A healing ministry conjures up pictures of Penecostal-type meetings, where faith healers whip their audiences up to a fevered emotional pitch, and people "claim their healing" and "swoon." Main line Christians are turned off by this sort of thing, and consequently tune out any interest in spiritual healing.

In observing faith healing services, I have seen too much emphasis placed on the faith of the sick person, rather than on the nature of the faithfulness of God, who loves and cares. Thus, if a person is not healed, he feels more depressed and more discouraged than ever. Evidently he "lacked the faith" and disappointed God, his family and his friends. Unfortunately, if there really is a lack of faith, it usually is on the part of those who prayed for the one who was sick.

I have also been bothered by faith healers who ask a sick person to believe in his healing and stop taking his medicine, as "proof" of his faith in being healed. A number of premature deaths have been caused this way. I also know that the power of mass hypnosis and the power of suggestion can, in the excitement and emotional fervor, cause a crippled person to throw

1. *Modern Man in Search of Soul.*

away his crutches and claim his healing, only to return home and find that he is still a cripple. Often he becomes a spiritual cripple, because he feels guilty for not having the faith to be healed.

I have talked with people who have gone to healing services, had the laying on of hands, swooned, and had others praying for their healing, and nothing happens. These people, seeking spiritual healing, are often put in the awesome position of being held responsible for producing and sustaining enough faith to be healed. There is no doubt that these and many other reasons can be held up as objections to spiritual healing. If no one was ever healed, there would be no reason to investigate the phenomenon. Yet, there are people who have had healings, not only of inner hurts and guilt, but also physical healings; and, yes, there have been cases of exorcism.

If we are to try to understand spiritual healing, then the best place to begin is in the examination of the problem of suffering. As good a place as any to start is with the classic story of suffering, that of Job. It is easy to understand how a wicked person would deserve to suffer, but Job was a righteous, God-fearing man, who was a good husband and good father to his seven sons and three daughters. Why, then, did he experience such endless suffering? Can a person make sense out of Job's afflictions?

When calamity came, it struck Job with a vengeance. Overnight, all his livestock were stolen, his servants were slain, and a tornado struck his eldest son's home, killing all ten of his children. Job responded to all of this by mourning his losses, but he also fell to the ground and worshipped God by saying, "The Lord gave and the Lord has taken away; blessed be the name of the Lord."[2] These words have often been quoted in prayers, but when Job said them, he believed that his suffering came from God, and that it would make sense in time.

Incredibly, Job's suffering continued. His body was afflicted with sores, from his toes to his head. He sat in the ashes and scraped his sores with a piece of broken pottery. His wife said to him, "Are you still holding on to your integrity? Curse God and die!"

Job responded by saying, "Shall we accept good from God, and not trouble?"[3]

Then three of Job's friends came to console him, but they believed that suffering was always in direct proportion to a person's wrongdoing. Secretly, under their pretense of comfort-

2. Job 1:21   3. Ibid., 2:9,10

103

ing and consoling, they believed that Job had fooled everyone about being such a good, God-fearing man. All they wanted to do was find out what Job's big sin was that had caused all his suffering. They advised Job to come clean and tell them what sin he had committed. After all, they were his friends. What are friends for?

When Job said that he had committed no sin to deserve such suffering, his friends, being such good friends, got frustrated with him. Eliphaz tried to brighten up Job by saying, "Behold, happy is the man whom God reproves; therefore despise not the chastening of the Almighty. For he wounds, but he binds up; he smites, but his hands heal."[4]

This kind of advice reminds me of the time my Uncle Stan was almost killed by a car accident and ended up in a body cast, in a great deal of pain. One day a woman, a regular Job's comforter, said to him, "Look on the bright side Stanley, something good will come of this!" I think he would have killed the woman, if he could have reached her!

For Job there was no bright side. He told off his friends, pointing out to them that the wicked seem to do all right in life, and they don't even believe in God. Job's suffering was so intense that he began to loathe the day he was born and longed for death. He even got mad at God for his silence and desertion. (But God can take us getting mad at him.) Finally, the silence was broken, and God spoke to Job. Job asked forgiveness, and God told Job's friends that they were wrong about his suffering. The whole point of the story of Job is to refute the belief that we suffer in direct relation to our sin. It also points out that suffering can be so terrible that we can wish we were dead, and at that point suffering makes no sense.

I believe the beginning of wisdom concerning the afflictions of life is to realize that when we try so hard to make sense out of them, we go nuts! Suffering doesn't make any sense—it is a fact of life. To gain a perspective on healing, one has to look at the problem of suffering and sickness. Unfortunately, too often a Christian looks at sickness as being sent from God to be his cross to bear in life, so he can suffer with Christ and grow as a Christian.

One time, a young Roman Catholic nun had tragedy and illness, one right after the other. Finally she went to her Mother Superior and said, "Why do I have all these afflictions?"

"Well," said the Mother Superior, "it is because God loves you

4. Ibid., 5:17,18

104

so much. He only gives suffering to those he loves, knowing they will bear it."

Whereupon the young nun said, "If that's the way he treats his friends, no wonder he has so few."

Suffer-the-afflictions-of-the flesh and be-of-good-cheer-faith does not lend itself to people feeling like they have permission to pray to God for healing of the flesh.

If sickness and suffering are from God, then the suffering person is in the rather dubious position of trying to pray to God to remove what he is doing in the first place. This view also raises a very interesting question: If sickness, suffering and death are God's will, then did Jesus go against God's will when he healed the sick and raised the dead?

When Paul brought the gospel to the Greek world, the Greek mind was programmed with the dualistic view of life that Plato and Socrates had taught. This view asserted that the body of man and the world of matter were evil. Inside the flesh of man was imprisoned an immortal soul that was pure and good. The soul was trapped inside the body, waiting to escape the prison of the flesh, so that it could go to the realm of Ideas. When Paul went to Greece to establish the Christian church, the holistic view of man in the Judeo-Christian tradition was contaminated with the dualistic view of the Greek philosophers.

Many of the early Christians tried to subdue the "evil flesh" and control their passions by retreating from the world. They left the cities, where women aroused the passions of lust in men, and lived in caves in the desert. There they punished the flesh by whipping their bodies with chains. Now, I happen to live through the heat of the desert every summer in Arizona, and I can tell you some of those so called holy men were not so holy as they were nuts!

People get confused about the will of God. The will of God means God is actively doing something that he intended to do. There is a real difference between God intending and God allowing certain things to happen, such as imperfections, disease and death, until his ultimate will is done. I cannot worship a God as a loving Father, who says on the one hand, "I love you," and then destroys a life by cancer, car accidents or drowning. How would you react if your neighbor intentionally drowned his six-month-old son and, when you asked him why, he replied, "Because I love him so much." You would want that man locked away for life, either for murder or insanity. Yet, how carelessly people explain disease and death by saying, "It's God's will. Just accept it."

I see God differently, as a God who loves to create, who is in the world, who loves, who heals, who does acts of power. In short, my God is not retired, much less dead. Sickness and death are enemies of God and man. That's what Christmas and Easter are all about to me.

Sickness and death are facts of life. The moment of inception brings with it the possibility of defects, disease and the promise of death. The same moment of inception is also the promise of life, the promise of joy, excitement, love, play, work and growth. When a loved one is struck down by death, we too often try to make some cosmic sense out of it. Why search for the why? Why search for the justice of it all, when life makes no sense? We cannot make sense out of tragedy. Life is not fair. It isn't fair that I was born in the United States, the greatest country in the world. It doesn't make sense that I was given many gifts and opportunities. It's not fair. I certainly can't look at someone less fortunate than I and say, "There, but for the grace of God, go I," as if God really loves me, but he sure clobbered that other poor guy.

When we read the Gospel of Mark we are confronted with the fact that it is a testament to the healing powers of Jesus. He came not just to save people from their sin, so they could be saved and go to heaven, but he came to heal the sick, raise the dead and perform mighty acts of power. The New Testament Church was carrying out Jesus' commission to the disciples to preach the Good News and to heal the sick.

What happened to the healing ministry of the Christian Church? When I was in seminary, I learned that the first century Christian Church needed signs from God, such as miraculous healings, in order to say to the world that this new faith is of God, who has the power to raise Jesus from the dead. After the church was established, God withdrew his power because it was no longer needed. The Christian Church was established. No need for healing after that. I find this very strange, because in every church, in every pew, there are people needing to be healed and made whole.

Someone once discovered that the reason birds fly is not because they have wings, but birds have wings because they fly. In the same manner, Christ did not forgive the sinner, heal the sick, and raise the dead to prove he was the Messiah. He did mighty works of love because he was God—a God so close that people could touch him, talk with him, have supper with him. People felt, experienced and knew of the great power of God's love, incarnate in Jesus. It created a turning point for those who experienced that love. The person was either completely changed by his love and became a new person, or he rejected that love because it was too costly, and ended up hating Jesus for giving him a glimpse of God and his love.

St. Augustine, in his early writings, claimed that healing had ceased in the church, and was no longer necessary. But in his later life he changed his mind, after hearing of 70 miracles attested to in his own diocease in two year's time. In 426 A.D., just three years before he died, he said that he was wrong about the age of miracles being past and described the miraculous cures which he had seen. He wrote, "Miracles do not happen in contradiction to nature, but only in contradiction to that which is known to us about nature."

In the book, *Life Together*, Dietrich Bonhoeffer writes:

> "Confess your faults one to another." (James 5:16) He who is alone with his sin is utterly alone. It may be that Christians, notwithstanding corporate worship, common prayer, and all their fellowship in service, may still be left to their loneliness. The final break-through to fellowship does not occur because, though they fellowship with one another as believers and as devout people, they do not fellowship as the undevout, as sinners. The pious fellowship permits no one to be a sinner. So everyone must conceal his sin from himself and from the fellowship. We dare not be sinners. Many Christians are unthinkably horrified when a real sinner is suddenly discovered among the righteous. So we remain alone with our sin, living in lies and hypocrisy. The fact is that we are sinners.[5]

If the healing of forgiveness cannot take place in the context of the church or in Christian fellowship, then how can the healing of physical afflictions take place?

What happened to the healing church? Does God love his people any less today than he did in the first century A.D.? The need for healing is still real. Has God turned the healing of illness over to the secular world of science and medicine, because they can perform even better "miracles"?

James Lynch in his book, *The Broken Heart*, writes:

> The adoption of scientific ways of thinking had far-reaching consequences for many aspects of society. One of its most dramatic influences occurred within formalized religion, especially

5. Dietrich Bonhoeffer, *Life Together* (New York: Harper & Brothers, 1954)

Christianity. Part of the driving force behind the growth of Christianity resided in the fact that it was a religion of healing. Christ was a healer; one of the transcribers of the New Gospel, Tucker, was a physician, and much of New Testament described miracles that involved the healing of disease. Until the twentieth century, healing was one of the most highly visible social functions of religion....

With the growth of scientific medicine in the twentieth century, two things occurred. First of all, people saw less need for this type of "magical" religious healing. Secondly, and perhaps of greater significance, churches themselves adopted objectivity as a means par-excellence for explaining their own beliefs. This latter stance of objectively assessing faith systems and theology, I believe proved to be an especially disruptive posture for religion, and one that had immediate consequences. These two changes brought about a dramatic decline in the healing aspects of religion, as well as a consequent decline in interest in religion itself.[6]

At a church celebration in the Vatican, there was a parade of all the pomp and wealth of the Roman Catholic Church. A Cardinal turned to the Pope and said, "No longer can the church say 'silver and gold have I none.'" "True," replied the Pope, "and neither can it say 'take up thy bed and walk.'"

I see the problem as an eternal conflict between "form" and "essence." By form, I mean the innate desire for man to structure his religious life, to organize it and develop all kinds of rules and regulations which provide an outward display of religiosity. Following the rules becomes the path of righteousness and salvation. If there isn't a rule, and you're in doubt, don't. Essence, on the other hand, is all energy and power. It is the power of creative growth. The relationship between God and man is open and dynamic. An essence person would agree with St. Augustine's rule, "Love God and do as you please."

The prophets and Jesus were people of essence. Their energy, truth and ability to speak to the hearts of men threatened the form people of formalized religion. Thus, the prophets were stoned, and Jesus was crucified. In the same way today, I wonder if the charasmatic movement of the Christian church, with its emphasis on healing people, is very threatening to the form people of organized Christianity. This is why it's so difficult to talk about and have people, reasonable people, investigate faith healing today.

If, then, I am to see spiritual healing in a new light, the starting point for me is what I believe about God. I believe in a God of love, whose love is not like anything between humans.

6. *The Broken Heart*

His love is scandalous, in that he loves the unlovable. He loves the ones least deserving of his love, as well as being a lover of the "good" people. Just think of it, God loves the murderer on death row, as well as the victim of his murder. He loved an Albert Schweitzer and an Adolph Hitler. Wait a minute, isn't that going too far? God couldn't love Hitler. Well, he loves all of his children, but he may not love what his children do with their lives. God gives man the freedom to say "yes" or "no" to his love. "For God so loved the world that he gave his one and only Son, that whoever believes in him shall not perish but have eternal life. For God did not send his Son into the world to condemn the world, but to save the world through him."[7]

Now if God is such a loving God, then why are not all people healed when they pray to this God of power and action? If he loves us so much, why is he so silent when we need him the most?

I have always been a fan of the writer, C. S. Lewis. After he wrote the book *The Problem of Pain,* where he focused in on the problem of suffering, his beloved wife died. The problem of pain became very personal, and all his brilliant reasoning was of no value. He, like Job, wailed in anguish and anger against God for taking his wife. As a writer, he wrote of his anger and pain, and eventually it was published under a pseudonym, because he was respected as a brilliant apologist for Christianity. How human this is for a Christian, especially a well-known one, to believe that God sent the suffering, and because of being in a position where others looked up to him, he was not supposed to reveal the great pain, the crushing blow, the anger and doubts.

Later on, the book, *A Grief Observed,* was published under Lewis' own name. Listen to his pain and anguish about God in these words:

> But go to Him when your need is desperate, when all other help is vain, and what do you find? A door slammed in your face, and a sound of bolting and double bolting inside. After that, silence. You may as well turn away. The longer you wait, the more emphatic the silence will become....
>
> Not that I am (I think) in much danger of ceasing to believe in God. The real danger is of coming to believe such dreadful things about Him. The conclusion I dread is not, "So there is no God after all," but "So this is what God's really like. Deceive yourself no longer...."
>
> There is no answer. Only the locked door, the iron curtain, the vacuum, absolute zero. "Them as asks don't get." I was a fool to ask.[8]

7. John 3:16,17
8. C.S. Lewis, *A Grief Observed* (New York: Seaburg Press, 1961)

One of the most difficult questions I was ever asked was by a nine-year-old girl who, through her tears, asked me, "I prayed to God to heal my Daddy. Why didn't he answer my prayer?"

I said to her, "God did answer your prayer and other prayers like yours a long time ago. In fact, about 2,000 years ago, God personally answered your prayer when he allowed his Son Jesus to suffer and die on a cross, so that on Easter the enemy of both God and man—death—would be defeated."

When a person turns in faith to a loving God, that act of faith will cast aside fear. To believe and know God's love casts out fear. For the sick person, to be surrounded by people who are accepting, loving and touching is a powerful experience. There is healing in touching and loving.

Dr. Raymond Moody, who interviewed hundreds of people who had an out of the body experience when they almost died, told of those who were met by a spiritual being—some knew that it was God. These people were not judged by God, but they saw the consequences of their acts toward other people. The only question people heard this spiritual being ask them was not, "What have you done with your life?" but, "Who have you loved?" This question made a profound influence on them when they returned to their bodies and carried on their lives.

I wonder if you are like me when it comes to prayer. I have said to a person, "I'll pray for you," and I haven't. I have also prayed for an answer, and then hedged my prayer with, "If it be Thy will." It's as if I really don't believe or expect an answer to my prayer but, "God, if you could possibly get around to answering my prayer, it will be fine." It's almost like the old story of the door-to-door salesman, who asked the person who answered the doorbell, "You don't want to buy a duck, do you?" I realize my prayer life has much to be desired, and I need the courage to pray with expectancy. Sometimes I feel just like the man who was brought before Jesus to be healed of deafness and a speech impediment. With a deep sigh, Jesus told him, "Ephphatha!" with means, "Be opened!"[9]

I am reminded of the time a preacher gave a powerful sermon to his congregation to pray to God with expectancy. He exhorted them to believe that God would answer their prayers. During the closing prayer, the preacher said, "Lord, we beseech Thee to hear us—" Whereupon a loud, deep voice filled the church with, "Yes, what is it?" The preacher died of a heart attack!

It seems like I will never have all the answers about God that I

9. *Can You Wait Till Friday?*

110

would really like, especially in the area of spiritual healing. I have read many books on the subject over the years, and the most helpful novels for me have been *Healing* and *The Power to Heal* by Francis MacNutt, a Roman Catholic priest with a healing ministry.

In the book *Healing*, Father MacNutt writes:

> Faith is important for healing! But if we, in our weakness do all we can, God will bless us far beyond our own merits. Our faith lies in the obedience of praying for the sick, despite our weakness, doing the best we can to show faith, the mercy of Christ. We need to take ourselves less seriously, and God more seriously.
>
> This is something that we must each discover! That in spite of our weakness, when we step forward and pray the prayer of healing, doing the best we can according to the faith that God has given us, God blesses us in abundance, beyond our merits—even beyond the power of our faith.[10]

In Father MacNutt's book, *The Power to Heal*, which he wrote four years after his first book, he says, "The most important thing I have learned in the past few years about praying for healing is that usually people are not completely healed by prayer, but they are improved." He states that at healing services we too often expect people to be healed now, and now he realizes that "prayer for healing is often a process. It requires time."

He further states, "The cruelest thing a minister of healing can do is to tell a person whose ailment has improved through his prayer, 'Now, you must believe that you are healed. To pray again would be for you to lack faith in God.' "[11]

I again admit there is much I need to learn about faith healing. I don't see spiritual healing as working against modern medicine, but working with medicine in the healing of the whole person. I have seen miracles of spiritual healing. I know those healings *could* have been coincidences, but someone has said, "A coincidence is when God performs a miracle and chooses to remain anonymous."

10. Mark 7:31-34

11. Francis MacNutt, *Healing* (Notre Dame, Indiana: Ave Maria Press, 1974)

111

# 15

## The Journey to Health

The most priceless possession you have is health. If you were worth a billion dollars, but were paralyzed with a stroke, you would jump at the chance to trade places with a person who had his health. You would offer that person your billion dollars to trade his life for yours. Not suprisingly, you probably wouldn't have any "takers." If health is such a pearl without price, do you ever wonder why people take such risks with it? Why do they continue to smoke too much (in spite of the surgeon general's warning), to eat far too much junk food, to drink alcohol excessively, to exercise so little and to rush around, never taking time to relax?

If you decide to make health a goal in your life, it will provide you with the direction and energy you need to reach that goal. You will not reach that goal overnight, but you will be on the journey to health. You don't have to make all the necessary changes at once, because what I am talking about is an inner conversion to a new, positive life-style. If health is our goal, then the most important thing to realize is that it is the journey to health that counts; we will each change along the way, at our own unique rate. Now, I am not talking about you becoming a fanatic. I know that a fanatic about anything—religion, politics, or health—can turn a person off rather than help him to make a meaningful change. Fanatics demand that we make drastic changes: too much is demanded too soon; therefore, we don't want to even try. A fanatic is like the person who prays, "God, I want patience, and I want it now!"

Let me share with you a little bit about my own journey to better health. I am now 49 years old, and I am healthier than I was when I was 35. At 35 I weighed 222 pounds, smoked over a pack of cigarettes a day, did not exercise, ate lots of refined sugar, knew nothing about nutrition or stress reduction , and I had high blood pressure. When I went back to graduate school at 35, I did not realize that I was starting on a journey to health.

Looking back, I know that my growth and progress would have been faster if I had consciously made a goal of health. In 1971, I was invited to be a lecturer at the first convention of the American Society for Preventive Dentistry, in Chicago. I knew very little about preventive dentistry, much less a preventive, holistic health model. But I wanted to be "in," so I purchased some dental floss, put it in my coat pocket, and let a little string of it casually hang out. I had no idea that my involvement as a psychologist in preventive dentistry would change my beliefs about health. I began to hear dentists talk about the dangers of refined sugar. Ridiculous, I thought. I knew sugar was bad for your teeth and caused dental decay, but detrimental to your health? I heard other dentists talking about the importance of good nutrition and taking vitamins and minerals, but after all, didn't we get those things in our daily diet? But the more I stayed around these preventive health people, the more I began to be curious about the role of refined sugar, diet and nutrition, and I slowly noticed that I was reading and thinking more about these things. I had begun to grow and change.

During the years I was on the board of directors for the American Society for Preventive Dentistry, I began to realize that the rest of the board members were changing. People who smoked quit. Refreshments served at meetings were fresh fruit and cheese. Weight was lost. Physical exercise became more and more a vital part of a person's life-style. I especially remember Dr. Bob Barkley who, before his death in a plane crash, was the most energetic, talented man I have ever known. He was "Mr. Preventive Dentistry." I can vividly remember him telling an audience that four years earlier he had gone to Dr. Ken Cooper's Clinic in Dallas. When he went he was thirty pounds overweight and he did not exercise. He told us, and I loved him for being so honest, that he didn't change immediately after going through the clinic, and that it took him four years before he lost that thirty pounds and began jogging regularly. It made me feel so much better that it took a genius like Bob Barkley four years to change. That meant there was hope for the rest of us.

At that time I did lose 37 pounds, but I gained back 30. I didn't realize that my weight problem was not a matter of going on a diet, but rather a need to change my eating life-style. As far as my smoking was concerned, I knew that it was just a temporary bad habit. I believed this so thoroughly, that I never bought a carton of cigarettes—I just bought a pack or two at a time. Finally I made the decision to quit smoking and to never smoke one cigarette, ever.

Now, at 49, my weight is between 190 and 195 pounds, which is what I weighed at 21. In regards to dieting, I have come to the conclusion that each person is unique in his own body chemistry and metabolism. Here is my sad story (doesn't everyone have a sad story about taking off weight and keeping it off?). I had read that if a person would just eliminate lunch, he would lose weight. So I eliminated lunch. Of course I knew that if you stopped eating rich, sugary desserts and refined sugar, you would lose weight. So I did that. And, naturally, one had to exercise vigorously for an hour a day to lose weight. I got in excellent physical condition. If you reduce your total caloric intake drastically, you will lose weight. I reduced my intake of calories drastically, and even stopped eating all fried foods. Ultimately, I realized that if you did all those things for a long time and you didn't lose any weight, you were going to get discouraged!

I began to see that there might be something else going on in my body. I started to experiment with adding or eliminating various foods, and I found that fruits like apples and oranges were causing me to not lose weight. I also found out that the very food that I would periodically get a craving for was dynamite for gaining weight. I didn't miss sugar and all those desserts, but I would crave Mexican food, a good pepperoni pizza, or Jeannie's lasagna. Thus I identified some nutritional areas which are troublesome for me. I have also discovered that fasting for two to four days at a time helps keep my weight down.

I basically live a life free of refined sugar as far as it is possible. It is very difficult to be completely free of refined sugar, when so much of it is hidden in our foods. It makes a "label reader" out of you, as so many food products have sugar added.

What is your life-style in regards to food? Have you thought about eliminating junk food, refined sugar, white flour and deep-fried foods? If you are wondering about the effect refined sugar has on your health, read *Sugar Blues* by William Duffy and *Sweet and Dangerous* by John Yudkin. Sugar is a major factor in dental disease, obesity, hypoglycemia, diabetes and suspected as a factor in heart disease and cancer. No wonder Gloria Swanson calls sugar, "poison."

I was recently able to hear Dr. Devis Burkitt when he lectured in Phoenix. He is in the practice of preventive medicine. He talked about the importance of oral fiber in our diets. He explained that the addition of fiber to the diet, either in the form of a tablespoon of bran, whole wheat bread, or cereal, would reduce the need for surgery for hemorrhoids by 60% to 70% and reduce the incidence of diverticulosis disease by 90%.

As far as the other changes in my life-style are concered, I have made many since that first exposure in 1971 to the world of holistic health. I now exercise on a regular basis for an hour a day at home, on my exercycle. It's not as much fun as jogging, but at least it's weatherproof, and I use the time to practice my visualization exercises for stress reduction. It is also an excellent time for me to talk things over with God. In addition, I do 100 leg lifts with weights on to keep the muscles in my damaged leg strong. It keeps my stomach muscles in shape! Traveling does interrupt my exercise routine, so I just do the best I can on the road, and pick up my regular routine when I get home.

I am finally able to practice the fine art of relaxing and doing nothing, and I must say I have learned to do it very well. One of my favorite sports is to pitch on the church softball team, in a slow-pitch league. It is a good change for me to approach a game as a time to have fun, and not to take it as a deadly serious, competitive sport.

I also have taken up skiing again, Before I damaged my left knee in football, I was learning how to ski on those old hickory skis that cost $15.00, with ski boots that cost $10.00 (the good old days!). They were so comfortable that I could move my feet around in those old boots real easy! I jokingly used to say that I have had only two skiing lessons: the first one on how to fall and the second one on how to fill up the hole.

Last winter I actually tried skiing with the new short skis and new boots. Before I went out, I prepared by visualizing myself flying down that mountain, allowing my skis and the snow to become as one. I wanted to test out that first day, because I knew that if I had too much pain in my left knee, I wouldn't be able to continue. I found myself actually doing what I had visualized, and there was only a little pain in walking the next day. I think that it is significant to add here that before I ever started on my physical exercise venture, my left knee was so weak that I could not even jump on it. It was like a dead knee. Not any more!

My personal journey to health will continue as I continue to have more fun growing and learning new ideas. I closed my private practice in March of 1975, and the past four and a half years have been the most exciting, productive and creative years of my life. The brain is just like a muscle; if you don't exercise it and feed it regularly, it will shrivel up and atrophy.

As I began to focus in on the goal of health, my perceptual

world changed. I suddenly "saw" new books and articles on health. They were really there all along, but it was not personally profitable for me at that time to perceive them. I realize that we are now experiencing a major revolution in health and preventive medicine.

It is ironic that this revolution in health, including everything from yoga to nutrition, exercise, and diets of high fiber is going on primarily outside the medical profession. More and more people are becoming aware that medically prescribed tranquilizers, such as Valium, have dangerous side effects, are addicting and often fatal when mixed with alcohol.

An article in *U.S. News and World Report* entitled "Do Doctors Hook Women on Drugs?" speaks to the issue:

> Women's addiction to legally prescribed drugs, often in combination with alcohol, is being exposed as a major public-health problem. As a result, Congress may move to require that prescription drug labels describe potential side effects. Among the findings of two mid-September Congressional probes:

> Roughly 60% of all drug related visits to hospital emergency rooms are made by women.

> The No. 1 drug that women take in overdoses is Valium, the U.S.'s most widely prescribed pill. New evidence suggests that the tranquilizer may be addictive even if taken only briefly.

> Eighty-five percent of women under treatment for drug problems have combined one mood-altering drug with another, or with alcohol.

> Doctors who don't specialize in psychological problems prescribe 97% of the mood drugs taken by women. Usually women are not advised of the side effects of the drugs.

> Representative Cardiss Collins (D-Ill.) claimed doctors are partly to blame for women's drug problems. "It is not uncommon," the Congresswoman said, "for a doctor to advise a male patient to work out his problem in the gym, or on the golf course, while a female patient with the same symptoms is likely to be given a prescription for Valium."[1]

I have asked a friend of mine in Seattle to tell her story of the struggle and turmoil she experienced for a year, while withdrawing from legally prescribed tranquilizers from her physician. She did not take massive dosages, but just followed her doctor's orders to take three to four pills a day. She was reassured that

1. "Do Doctors Hook Women on Drugs?" (*U.S. News and World Report*, September 24, 1979)

these pills would not be harmful or addicting for her. Here is her story:

"Today I am happier and more content than I have been in years. I have a good job, good health, and three wonderful children. Being single after 20 years of marriage is not as bad as I thought it would be; in fact, it has some great rewards. It hardly seems possible that just one year ago my main goal was to survive each day; many times it seemed as if life just wasn't worth the effort.

"It's amazing how I rationalized for almost four years that the daily pills I took were O.K.; I figured they were actually good for me. When I look back I wonder how it happened, and yet I know. I had been under a great deal of stress. We had moved to Seattle, Washington, after ten years of marriage, children, close friends, church activities and volunteer work, all in the same community. Leaving deep ties of friendship and a home that I loved was very hard for me. I had also done a daily radio program for homemakers on a local Christian radio station and found the work immensely satisfying. Even though I faced a difficult adjustment, I had ten years of a happy marriage behind me. I was hardly ever sick and felt full of energy. The future looked bright enough, but after the move, things began to change.

"The details of the next few years really need not be shared, for who can say exactly why a marriage falls apart? For everyone this happens to, it becomes a very personal and painful experience. As these events unfolded in my life, my disposition began to change drastically. I was irritable and crabby. My mood swings were unpredictable, and I began to experience some physical symptoms that scared me. Suddenly I would get dizzy, and my heart would start beating faster. I learned much later that this was caused by anxiety. The stress I was experiencing caused some physical problems, and I subsequently went through two hospital visits for tests.

"When my doctor could find no physical reasons for my health problems, he finally suggested tranquilizers. I rebelled at this suggestion, because I didn't believe in drugs of any kind. I seldom even took an aspirin. I remember the day he looked at me with great concern and told me that the stress I was going through could cause all kinds of problems like high blood pressure, strokes and heart attacks. He said, 'Bev, you had better get rid of whatever it is in your life that is causing you so much stress.'

117

"I went home that day and reluctantly began taking tranquil-izers. At first, I only took them when I felt I needed them, but after awhile I discovered that if I took two or three on a daily basis, those awful attacks of anxiety and fear rarely happened.

"In October of 1975, I met Dr. Ken Olson. It was an encounter that was to change the entire course of my life, but not for several years. It's funny how you can listen to someone, but not really hear them. Ken was a guest on my daily radio program on KGDN in Edmonds, Washington. It was one of the best inter-views I ever had.

"After the show, we went to lunch. When we got seated, he looked at me very seriously and said, 'Okay, Bev, what's bother-ing you?' I was shocked because I thought I had covered up everything quite well. After spilling out about 45 minutes worth of all my miseries and woes, Ken said, 'You really enjoy being miserable, don't you?'

'No!' I sputtered.

'Well, you sure are doing everything to insure it,' Ken answered.

"I was stunned, but I never forgot those words—except, like all things, change comes over a long period of time. Instead of meeting my problems head on and learning how to face myself, I kept on taking tranquilizers as my doctor suggested.

"In a short time my entire world seemed to crumble. I often look back and wonder how much the regular use of tranquilizers contributed to the final break-up of my marriage. I know they kept me in a 'blah' state. I never really felt anything. I didn't laugh very often and I couldn't cry. I thought it was because I was going through so much emotional pain that I had become numb, but I was really medicated beyond feeling.

"After several separations, reconciliations and marriage counseling, the decision was made to divorce. This was a devas-tating blow for me, because I had always believed that Chris-tians didn't get divorced. I wonder if I'd had all my faculties, I would have fought harder to save my marriage.

"For a year after the divorce, I went around feeling just like a zombie. The only easy thing to do was to take more pills. I just existed, going through the motions of living. I hated the respon-sibility of working and running a home all by myself. I was filled with bitterness and resentment. Later, I found out that most of those feelings were normal, and that I should have worked them out instead of running and hiding behind pills, pills and more

118

pills. Looking back, I realize that I was not aware of how much trouble I was in.

"I went to work as a hostess on a daily telephone talk show in Seattle. I'm sure my acting ability was so great that only those who were closest to me knew what I was going through. I was good at making others think everything was just fine, and that I had it all together.

"During the years that followed, I sponsored several seminars with Ken Olson. I would sit and listen with rapt attention to everything he said, again believing but not applying. The turning point came, though, when he came to do a special seminar entitled, 'Hurts, Healing and Wholeness.' There might as well not have been anyone else at that seminar; I was sure every word was for me. I suddenly saw what I was doing to myself and my family, and I realized that I had to get off tranquilizers.

"Every time I had tried to quit taking tranquilizers had been a disaster: I would have a sudden return of all the symptoms that I had taken them for in the first place, only much worse. I had a long talk with Ken, and he explained that one of the most important things was not just to quit 'cold turkey.' Because of the possibility of convulsions and death, most people going off drugs check themselves into a hospital.

"After our talk, I decided that I would gradually go off tranquilizers at home, since I had not only the help of Ken by long distance telephone, but I had also changed doctors, and my new doctor was a wonderful man who directed the counseling at Schick Shadle Hospital for Alcoholism in Seattle. Peter Tighe was an expert on addiction and understood that emotional dependency could be stronger than physical dependency. With this kind of help, I entered into the adventure with excitement! I was certainly not prepared for what was about to happen to me. I went on a six-weeks gradual withdrawl program.

"Unfortunately, the symptoms started the very first week, with a low-grade headache and on and off feelings of irritability. When I visited my doctor, he said, 'Well Bev, now the real you comes out. Now you'll find out whether or not you can cope with the ups and downs of life.' I had been medicated beyond feeling for so long, I didn't know what 'normal' was.

"To say the next few months were a nightmare would be an understatement. I'm not sure how many times I considered going back to tranquilizers—at least once or twice a day. By the third week, I was starting to wake up several times a night, and still had the headache. The smallest problems seemed like giants; my ability to cope with them was practically nill. During the fourth week, I was really wondering if it was worth it. The awful anxiety attacks started. If you have ever had one, you can't imagine how frightening they can be. I would suddenly feel like I couldn't breathe, then my heart would start racing, and I would start to shake and begin to get dizzy. There was pain and pressure in my chest. I felt sure I was dying and would be terribly afraid. After it was all over, I felt shaken and weak. Some of the attacks were severe, some were not so severe. All of them were frightening. When the fifth week rolled around, I could hardly concentrate on anything, and I was waking up in the early morning, unable to go back to sleep again, as well as waking up several times during the night. I'm sure this lack of good sleep didn't help matters.

"During this time I was still doing my daily one-hour talk show. No one knew what misery it was for me to get through that one hour. I would have such severe anxiety that I would watch the clock every minute, wondering every day if I would make it through the hour. I was terrified that I would pass out during the show. It's funny how fear builds up, and you never stop to realize that the thing you are so afraid of never happens. When the show was over, I would go home and crawl into the safety of my bed. There I felt hidden from the world and secure. I didn't go out much; most of my energy went into my own survival.

"Finally Ken Olson got through to me that vitamins were important, and I began to take large doses of vitamin C and a B complex. Because stress robs the body of calcium and potassium, he had me take those also. I wish I had started sooner. I also learned that alcohol prolongs withdrawl. It is tempting to have a glass of wine when things get unbearable, but alcohol is a drug too, and one dependency can be traded for another.

"The worst of the hell was over, and the job of rebuilding my life was before me, but I knew that I had six months to a year before I would be normal again. The only thing that kept me going was the hope that I would be whole again. I thank God that I had a wonderful doctor who let me call him anytime with my complaints. He would patiently explain to me what was happening and assure me that I was going to be okay—time and time again. It was a miracle he didn't get tired of me.

"As I began to heal, I realized that I could do a few things for myself. When you are at the bottom, people can tell you what to do, but sometimes you can't muster up the strength to do anything but exist. But finally, one day, you want to start crawling out, and you begin to do things. Walking is one of the greatest things to start with. It really helps the body and the mind. Also, good nutrition is a must. Sugar poisons the body and the emotions. When I began to eat three, well-balanced meals a day, I was amazed how it helped.

"The real change came when Ken insisted that I get a hair analysis, because I wasn't healing fast enough. I found out through the test that I was low in iron, zinc, potassium and two other trace minerals. After taking these for just one week, I felt like a new person. I haven't been tired or depressed since.

"Now, a little over a year later, I feel better than ever. I am taking care of my body and my emotions. I have a new job, and I love it. I work long hours and have lots of energy. My family is closer than we have ever been, and I really am grateful to my three children for their support. We all are a lot stronger from the experience. Being at the bottom is bleak and lonely, but climbing back up to the top is not only magnificent, but you sure feel proud of yourself.

"The biggest thing that pulled me through was my faith in God. I knew that through it all he loved me and accepted me just as I was. I felt his love and strength, even when things were darkest. In fact, several times I would cry out in utter desperation, 'God, are you there?' and immediately something tangible would happen to let me know that, yes, he was there, caring and always will be."

In July of 1979, the federal government reported that Americans, although generally healthier than ever, are killing themselves needlessly through smoking, drinking, poor diet and preventable accidents. The study stated that deaths from degenerative diseases, such as heart ailments, stroke and cancer, have increased sharply and now account for 75% of all U.S. deaths. Accidents of all types are the leading cause of death up to the age of forty.

Some of the main points of "The Surgeon General's Report on Health Promotion and Disease Prevention" were:

Cigarette smoking is the single most preventable cause of death.

Alcohol is a factor in more than 10% of all U.S deaths.

Many Americans are "apathetic and unmotivated" toward better health, often viewing illness as a matter of random choice, not to be overted but to be tolerated and accepted.

Personal life-styles are responsible for a large share of unnecessary disease and disability in the United States.

Americans are eating too much sugar, salt, red meat, fat and cholesterol and not enough whole grains, cereals, fruits, vegetables, fish, poultry and legumes.

Adults should be encouraged to exercise vigorously, if possible, at least three times a week for about 15 to 30 minutes, each time.

Up to 20% of all cancer deaths may be linked to exposure to chemicals and other hazards on the job.

Injuries, many preventable through adherence to speed limits and use of seat belts, amount to half of all deaths between the ages of 15 and 24.

The report called for a second public health revolution to stem the death toll from heart disease, cancer and accidents, much in the same way that polio, tuberculosis and other infectious diseases were tamed in the past. It urged that the national health strategy be dramatically recast to emphasize disease prevention through life-style changes and personal conduct as well as medical advances.[2]

Did you know that in 1900, coronary heart disease was an unknown factor? Dr. Paul Dudley White, who graduated from medical school in about 1911, says that he had never seen a coronary heart patient in his training. Now I have a funny feeling that the "good old days" were not such easy days. Have you ever gone back and looked at the old family albums of grandmas and grandpas? The pictures! Oh my gosh, grim, life was grim; you wonder if anybody ever smiled. And it was tough. I don't think it was easy coming across the United States in a covered wagon, when your big day was 15 miles. And I don't think the women exactly enjoyed chewing dust, living in those little wagons, having kids and Indians around, and working from dawn 'til dusk. They had a life, in those early years, that was very grim and very hard. So how come they didn't have coronaries?

In the early 1900s we began to refine wheat. And when we refined wheat, we took out our natural source of vitamin E. That's right, just a small change in life-style. The importance of vitamin E in the prevention of blood clots, and in breaking them up after they do form, is now known.

The life-styles of thirty-five young executives and professors whose chief complaints were chest pains and fatigue were stud-

2. United Press International, "Report Calls for Crusade of Preventive Medicine" (*The Arizona Republic,* Sunday, July 29, 1979)

ied by Dr. John McCaury. Serious coronary problems were suspected in each case; however, their resting electrocardiograms were normal and there were no problems of high cholesterol levels. Yet each one of these men, ages twenty-five to forty, showed tense chest muscles. As their way of life was investigated, all showed the following pattern:

> More than thirty of them smoked, they averaged an intake of two cups of coffee or tea daily. They all suffered from poor posture. They all overworked, putting in twelve to twenty hours a day. They had no exercise. They all had very unsatisfactory diets. They were bending over most of the day. Every one of these points was matter of life-style, and each was a susceptibility factor.

As these men began to examine their life patterns and consider the ramifications on their health, the following changes were made, with remarkable results:

> They stopped drinking coffee and alchohol; they stoped eating spices and heavy foods. Those who smoked cut down to less than a pack a day, with the ultimate goal in mind of quitting completely. They reduced their work day. They introduced stretching exercises into their routines and initiated walking programs. Every single one of them stopped having chest pains.[3]

The journey to health begins by accepting personal responsibility for staying healthy. It means examining your life-style and deciding what you would like to change first. Stopping smoking will add years to your life. One of the best psychological benefits of regular exercise is not only getting a healthier body, but also feeling a positive sense of well-being and pride in getting into good physical condition again. Remember, exercise is also a marvelous counter-attack against depression.

Where you start and how fast you travel on your journey to health is up to you. If you backslide, don't get down on yourself, just get back on the road again. The basic question is this: health or sickness? It's whatever you decide.

> *There is a time to hurt,*
> *a time to heal,*
> *and a time to live.*
> *That time is now!*

---

3. John C. McCaury and James Presley, *Human Life Styling* (New York: Harper and Row, 1957)

# Appendix A

## Basic Steps for Visualization and Deep Relaxation

Sit in a comfortable chair, with your arms and legs uncrossed. Now begin to take some deep breaths, inhaling through your nose and exhaling through your mouth. Under stress our breathing becomes shallow, so after doing this for a short time, you will notice your breathing becoming much slower and your body beginning to relax.

Next, roll your eyes back in their sockets until you feel them hurt, and then let them go back to normal. Close your eyes and visualize the muscles in your forehead being pulled very tight. Then see the muscles becoming very limp, like a rubber band. Become aware of the warmth in your muscles and an increasing feeling of heaviness. Allow your body to make you aware of those areas where the muscles are tense; then let the muscle go and relax, becoming very limp and heavy. Now begin to count down from ten to one, saying to yourself, "With each number that I say and each breath that I take, I will relax even more and feel the heaviness of warmth and relaxation."

When you reach the number one, I want you to visualize yourself walking on the beach by the ocean. See yourself walking in the sand, feeling relaxed, smelling the salt air, feeling the wind caressing your face. You watch the sea gulls flying in the breeze so effortlessly and listen to their cries. You sit down on the beach, feeling the sand between your toes and fingers. The warmth of the sun feels so good and relaxing. You can hear the sound of the surf pounding, as each wave breaks and spills the foamy salt water up on the beach and then retreats once again into the sea. There is a timelessness to the sea. Your breathing is in harmony with the coming and going of the sea, and you are experiencing the feeling of complete peace.

Now relax even more and let any thoughts just pass on through your mind, as you see yourself relaxing and letting go. Let go of what you need to let go of—tension, hurts, bitterness and frustrations. You have permission to let go of whatever you need to. The feeling of inner peace and relaxation will stay with you. It feels so good to stop the world and relax. Each time you practice your relaxation and visualization, you will be able to relax more quickly and visualize more clearly whatever you want to see. You can keep on relaxing even more and seeing the changes you want to have. When it's time for you to come back from your relaxation and visualization, you will be able to do so by counting back up from one to three, and at the count of three you will open your eyes and feel very refreshed.

# Appendix B

## Visualization Exercise
## Getting in Touch With Your Emotions
## and Hurts of Yesterday

First, go through the visualization and deep relaxation exercise, but instead of seeing yourself on the beach, I want you to imagine that you are in a very beautiful building. Create the design of the building. Think about what it looks like. Is it made of stone, wood, steel? Does it have stained glass windows, leaded windows?

After you have visualized what the building looks like, picture a table in the center of the room. Drape it with whatever kind of beautiful cloth you want. Now see a spotlight shining down on top of the table. It is giving out a warm, yellow light. See yourself walking up to the table with your arms full of small boxes. In these boxes are all the hurts in your life. There may be a box of rejection, one of bitterness, resentment, fears, hates. They are each filled with painful memories of long ago. Some are filled with painful happenings of very recent times.

As you reach the table, take all the boxes filled with hurt and pain and put them down underneath the beautiful yellow light shining down from the ceiling. Now see yourself walking away from the table to a safe distance and sitting down in a comfortable chair. Relax in the chair and then look at all those hurts, all those painful memories, and ask yourself, "What hurts most now?" Wait for an answer from your subconscious mind. It may come to you as a shifting of muscle tension and a release of energy as you think about each item on the table. When you find that one thing that is hurting you the most, ask yourself, "Am I missing something? Is there something I am blocking out or not wanting to face?" If you discover a deeper level of pain from a supressed memory, relax and let the pain drain away. Focus on as much hurt as you feel comfortable with. Then let them go.

Now, from the safe distance of your chair, focus on the boxes of pain on the table. Begin to see and feel how free, how happy, how relieved you could be if you now got up and turned your back on them and walked away. See yourself walking away from the

127

table, leaving all those boxes with the light shining down on them.

You can vary and enlarge upon this theme of visualization in any way that makes it more effective for you. One woman saw herself walk up to the table and push all the boxes off into a large garbage can, which she then took outside and left for the garbage collectors.

# Appendix C

## On Overcoming Phobic Fears

Fear is a cruel tyrant which enslaves many people. Phobic fears are not just ordinary fears, but exaggerated, illogical fears. A phobic fear is walking down a sidewalk, hearing a jet plane flying over your head, and suddenly being struck with terror that it will fall out of the sky and hit you.

Joseph Wolpe and Arnold Lazarus teach a systematic way to densensitize a person's fears through relaxation and visualization. The person is asked to develop a list of ten fears, ranking them from 1-12, according to the intensity of the fear. The twelfth fear is the least feared one. When the person is deeply relaxed, he is asked to visualize the least feared experience. If he does not feel anxious about that fear, he can move up and visualize the next fear. If this fear causes great anxiety, then he stops and relaxes deeply. As deep relaxation is incompatible with fear, the fear loses some of its power. Finally, a person is able to visualize that number one fear and feel no anxiety.[1]

I have also suggested that people give their fears a funny name and then create a ridiculous situation in their imaginations that causes them to laugh at the fear. Spinoza said, "I saw that all the things I feared had nothing good or bad in them *except* insofar as my mind is affected by them."

---

1. Joseph Wolpe, *Psychotherapy by Reciprocal Inhibitions* (Stanford, California: Stanford University Press, 1958); Joseph Wolpe and Arnold A. Lazarus, *Behavior Therapy Techniques* (New York: Pergamon Press, 1966)

# Appendix D

## An Exercise to Express Emotions

One of the reasons we have a difficult time in expressing how we feel emotionally is that we don't take time to graphically describe how we feel. We have not learned to use descriptive language. For example, when someone says, "How are you feeling?" we answer, "I'm feeling lonely." "Feeling lonely" doesn't tell them *how* lonely we are feeling.

One husband in a seminar was trying to find words to express his love for his wife. He stuttered and stammered around, saying, "My love for you is like—ah—my feelings of love are—" But then he finally hit pay dirt when he said, "My love for you is like a boomerang; I throw it to you and it always comes back to me with more love." Now that's real!

Here are some samples of how lonely a person can be:

I'm so lonely that I feel just like I am at a cocktail party and I don't know one single person.

I'm so lonely that it feels like I've been away from you for a month, living in smelly motel rooms and eating one meal after another all by myself.

I'm so lonely that I feel like I'm 86 years old, trapped in an old county nursing home with the smell of urine everywhere. I feel like I have bed sores, no one visits me, and I have nothing to look forward to except death. No one cares if I'm alive or dead. I am useless. And I can't even die to end the loneliness.

Here are some exercises to help you begin to fully express your emotions. As you fill in the blanks, try to express the varying intensity and power of your emotions.

1. I'm so lonely

2. I'm so angry

3. I'm so sad

4. I'm so happy

5. I'm so depressed

6. My love for you is

# Appendix E

## Are You a Type A or Type B Personality?

Rate yourself on the following statements with a scale of 1-5, with 5 indicating that you are most like the statement.

| Type A Personality | | Type B Personality | |
|---|---|---|---|
| 1. Lack of self-approval | ___ | 1. Self-acceptance | ___ |
| 2. Raised with conditional love | ___ | 2. Raised with unconditional love | ___ |
| 3. Competitive | ___ | 3. Creative | ___ |
| 4. Impulsive | ___ | 4. Reflective | ___ |
| 5. Aggressive | ___ | 5. Productive | ___ |
| 6. Life by the number | ___ | 6. Non-workaholic | ___ |
| 7. Workaholic | ___ | 7. Many interests other than work | ___ |
| 8. Impatient | ___ | 8. Trust of self and others | ___ |
| 9. Intense | ___ | 9. Delegates responsibilities | ___ |
| 10. Few interests | ___ | 10. Patient | ___ |
| Score: | ___ | Score: | ___ |

If you score heavily in the Type A personality, take a look at the behaviors listed and decide which one of the areas you want to change first. Don't feel you have to do them all at once. That is a part of the Type A's problem! Remember, the goal is in changing. Set a period of time in the future, like six months, and rate yourself again. If you are married, I'm sure your wife or husband would like to rate you, as well as themselves. Remember, the goal of changing from a Type A personality to a Type B is to prevent a coronary!

# Buy From:
# Book and Health Food stores

Save Postage

**or order from:**

O'SULLIVAN
WOODSIDE
& COMPANY

2218 East Magnolia
Phoenix, Arizona 85034

| PLEASE SHIP AT ONCE: | copies | each | extension |
|---|---|---|---|
| Put Your Mind & Body in Order (CASETTE) | | @ 6.95 | $ |
| I Hurt Too Much For a Band-Aid | | @ 4.95 | |
| The Art of Hanging Loose | | @ 3.95 | |
| Can You Wait Till Friday? | | @ 3.95 | |

Please add 75¢ per copy for postage & handling

ENCLOSED IS MY ☐ CHECK ☐ CASH FOR ......$

Please Remit in U.S. Dollars

NAME _____

STREET ADDRESS _____

CITY _____

STATE _____ ZIP _____

# Buy From:
## Book and Health Food stores

Save Postage

### PLEASE SHIP AT ONCE:

| | copies | each | extension |
|---|---|---|---|
| Put Your Mind & Body in Order (CASETTE) | ___ | @ 6.95 | $ ___ |
| I Hurt Too Much For a Band-Aid | ___ | @ 4.95 | ___ |
| The Art of Hanging Loose | ___ | @ 3.95 | ___ |
| Can You Wait Till Friday? | ___ | @ 3.95 | ___ |

**Please add 75¢ per copy for postage & handling**

ENCLOSED IS MY ☐ CHECK ☐ CASH FOR.....$ ___

Please Remit in U.S. Dollars

**or order from:**

Ⓦ O'SULLIVAN
WOODSIDE
& COMPANY

2218 East Magnolia
Phoenix, Arizona 85034

NAME _____

STREET ADDRESS _____

CITY _____

STATE _____ ZIP _____